SUDDENLY SINGLE
AT SIXTY

Jo Peck grew up in Healesville, Victoria. She worked in advertising for thirty-five years, co-running her own ad agency, Working Girls Advertising, for twenty of those years. She lives in Melbourne with her new partner.

Suddenly Single at Sixty

Jo Peck

t

TEXT PUBLISHING MELBOURNE AUSTRALIA

The Text Publishing Company acknowledges the Traditional Owners of the country on which we work, the Wurundjeri people of the Kulin Nation, and pays respect to their Elders past and present.

textpublishing.com.au

The Text Publishing Company
Wurundjeri Country, Level 6, Royal Bank Chambers, 287 Collins Street, Melbourne Victoria 3000 Australia

Copyright © Jo Peck, 2024

The moral right of Jo Peck to be identified as the author of this work has been asserted.

All rights reserved. Without limiting the rights under copyright above, no part of this publication shall be reproduced, stored in or introduced into a retrieval system, or transmitted in any form or by any means (electronic, mechanical, photocopying, recording or otherwise), without the prior permission of both the copyright owner and the publisher of this book.

Published by The Text Publishing Company, 2024

Cover design by W. H. Chong
Cover images by LinaDes/iStock
Page design by Rachel Aitken
Typeset in Sabon LT Pro 12.5/19pt by J&M Typesetting

Printed and bound in Australia by Griffin Press, a member of the Opus Group. The Opus Group is ISO/NZS 14001:2004 Environmental Management System certified.

ISBN: 9781923058064 (paperback)
ISBN: 9781923059061 (ebook)

A catalogue record for this book is available from the National Library of Australia.

The paper this book is printed on is certified against the Forest Stewardship Council® Standards. Griffin Press, a member of the Opus Group, holds chain of custody certification SCS-COC-001185. FSC® promotes environmentally responsible, socially beneficial and economically viable management of the world's forests.

In memory of my mum, Olive

Suddenly Single at Sixty is a true story: it's my truth, and I have retold it as I experienced it, though others, whose names have been changed, may remember it differently. I make no excuse for that—everyone will have their own version of the facts.

PART 1

Annihilation

It's Saturday morning of the Queen's Birthday long weekend and we're about to go into the city to buy a birthday present for our godson, Jaran. While I wait for Rex to come downstairs, I look out with satisfaction over our newly landscaped back garden. The fresh sods of Sir Walter turf, yet to settle, the espaliered crabapple on the shed wall, more wire than foliage right now, the three-staked magnolias along the fence line and the bluestone paving, which was an especially hard-fought victory for me.

We'd long agreed that the garden needed a makeover, we just couldn't agree on what that might look like and Rex was loath to spend money 'unnecessarily'. Eventually I found a landscape designer attached to a garden centre who would produce a plan for free if we agreed to buy the plants and materials from the garden centre. She came back with a beautiful concept and I knew that Rex liked it too, but where he had envisaged a timber deck, the designer had suggested bluestone paving, which I agreed was a more natural fit. This became a major sticking point and stalled the process for months, Rex using cost to bolster his argument (assuming the bluestone would be more expensive), me thinking he was probably right, but for once holding out and hoping that this time I could be the one to decide what we spent our money on. Finally, to break the deadlock, I got the concept quoted both ways, and prepared, as usual, to capitulate. To our mutual surprise, the timber required some very expensive footings, and two different quotes from two different suppliers favoured the bluestone by a significant margin. Today, on this cold Melbourne morning, the view from the living room is a little stark and dreary, the freshly laid bluestone crudely conspicuous without its softening patina, but hope is planted and spring is coming.

Rex arrives and looks ready to go. He's got his city clothes on. A tartan wool scarf I gave him for his birthday last year and the khaki suede jacket we bought, after many cups of mint tea and much gesticulating, at the Grand Bazaar in Istanbul. To convince us it was leather the stallholder had used his fingers to simulate horns and run around his stall stomping and charging at us like a bull. Rex looks handsome, but not totally at peace. Something in his face suggests he'd rather be somewhere else. Nevertheless, I decide to test my luck and suggest that we might look at a new TV while we're in town. I prepare myself for the default response of 'No'. I'm ready for disappointment—that's usual when the suggestion is not his idea—but I'm not ready for the violence of his reaction.

'We don't need a fucking new TV. We have two perfectly good TVs already.'

Yes, I think, but they're both from TV's Jurassic age. I'm tired of Robson Green's *Extreme Fishing* adventures and reruns of *Midsomer Murders*. And hearing at work about all the great new Netflix series that I'm missing out on.

'You're so needy, never satisfied. Never happy,' he says.

Whether from the unfairness of that comment or the sudden wrenching spasm I feel in my gut, silent tears start to wet my cheeks.

'What are you crying for? It's only a TV.'

Instinctively, softly, I say, 'Somehow, I don't think this is only about a TV, Rex.'

Those words, born of innocence, or was it wilful ignorance, change everything. Rex stops yelling, collapses heavily into an armchair and simply stares out the back window onto the fledgling garden.

The weight of his silence presses in on me, crushing. The actual wait is interminable, giving me time to inventory the familiar room where I now sense a major drama is about to play out. The large faux Rothko painted by a friend before we were married, which has travelled with us to every house since, the vintage Polish film poster on the opposite wall, the circular tufted rug, a calming pool of pale sea green in the centre of the room, now with ever-present smattering of blond dog hair, the dancing ladies beginning to wilt in the black and white vase gifted to us by friends who minded our house while we were away, the once-beautiful Italian chaise sofa now pulled and clawed by pets whose trespasses were always easily forgiven, the space we share most nights while we attempt to watch the troublesome TV. Our lovingly curated living room.

Finally, without turning to look at me, he speaks: 'I'm seeing someone else.'

And there it is.

This is two weeks after our twenty-fifth wedding anniversary.

Four weeks after my sixtieth birthday.

When we were on the cusp of finally finishing work and pushing the 'Go' button on our retirement plans to take off and travel the world. Plans we had been making all our married life.

My thoughts tumble and trip over each other and fight to be first out my mouth. But do I even want to know? Who? Why? Why now? What does this mean for us, for our marriage? I want to hit rewind, not even mention the TV. Get on the tram, talk instead about what we might buy for Jaran, whether we might catch a movie at the Kino before we head home. But of course, I have to know. I can't pretend I didn't hear what he just said.

I'm seeing someone else. Four small words. So vast.

Finally, I ask the question that will carry the most weight on the outcome of this unwanted conversation: 'Do you love her?'

'Whatever that is—yes, I guess I do.'

I'm sixty and the husband I thought I'd be buried with is in love with someone else.

'Does this mean our marriage is over?'

'Well, I wouldn't put the house on the market just yet.'

I'm not even sure what that means, but at least it doesn't sound like a knock-out punch. If we're not selling up, maybe we're not splitting up. Maybe our marriage is salvageable yet.

Blindly I press on. 'Do I know her?'

'Yes.'

I steel myself. Equally wanting and not wanting to know. Please don't let it be a friend.

'Who?'

'Anna.'

Anna?

Surely not. But we only know one Anna—so it must be bland little Anna from the bowling club. Anna who wears sensible sandals, long frocks and works in an op shop? Anna who looks frightened every time I talk to her? Well, I guess that makes sense to me now—but, to be fair, she looks frightened when anyone tries to talk to her. Anna who is timid to the point of vanishing, or was, until at the urging of one of the senior lady members she surprised us all by performing an excruciatingly off-key highland fling at the bowling club Christmas party, while Rex and I nudged each other in the ribs, laughing conspiratorially. Now I wonder, was he seeing her even then? Was he humouring me to protect their secret? I couldn't be more floored. Anna is not Rex's type at all. She couldn't be more different from me. But maybe that's just the point. If he's tired of me, why would he choose someone similar? Even so, I wonder, what's the attraction? From where I sit, which is suddenly a very undesirable place, she seems to have one major thing going for her. She is very good at bowls. Club champion. That and the fact that she is thirty-four, compared to my sixty.

I want to lash out. I want to take the sharpest knife from the block on the kitchen bench behind me and stick it through his cheating heart. But the most hurtful thing I can spit out is: 'My next partner will be so much more emotionally evolved than you.' Who knows where that came from? What changed my impulse from murder to one-upmanship? It is my natural competitiveness kicking in, or my need for self-preservation, for in truth I felt the exact opposite. I felt totally washed up as a woman and permanently disfigured by embarrassment.

My husband is a cliché. And, suddenly, I am reduced to a cliché's wife.

He's sixty-two, and he's having an affair—correction, he's 'in love'—with a girl young enough to be his child. He tells me he's tried to stop it. They both have. At that, my jealousy jumps right down a rabbit hole. I've been told that it only started at Christmas time, five months ago, but is that long enough to have been on again and off again, maybe a number of times? Is that long enough to fall in love with someone, when you can only see each other in snatched illicit bursts? Crucially, is that long enough to decide to overthrow a twenty-five-year relationship that finally seemed to be past its biggest hurdles?

Ours was never what you'd describe as an easy or smooth relationship. It had weathered many storms, but I finally felt we were sailing into clear air.

He says he knows that for him it will spell 'social, financial and emotional suicide'. His exact words. Which means he has weighed the impact of those massive hits and still chosen her. He says the attraction is just too strong. But as I sit, mostly silent, absorbing these devastating blows, I can't help wondering whether it's the attraction that's too strong, or simply the male vanity of being validated and adulated by a pretty young thing that is irresistible to him. Anna is not a girl you'd describe as gorgeous, and until now I would never have even thought to be envious of her, but she does have some of those cues that men seem to find appealing: long wavy hair, small features, downcast brown eyes and a shyness that invites protection. There is something old fashioned and naive about her. She could be easily cast in a Jane Austen film. Nevertheless, she is not in *Pride and Prejudice*; she is right here playing a major part in the bust-up of my life, so perhaps not so naive after all. And one thing I know for certain is that this fresh-faced girl is something that I, at sixty, with no mystery left in me, simply can't compete with.

The talking has stopped and the pain has kicked in. As visceral bolts of shock pinball from my brain to my gut to my bowels, I don't know if I will faint, throw up or shit myself. In the end, I do none of those things. I surprise myself by not even crying. Perhaps because I can't process what I have just heard. The implications are unthinkable, too big to contain, too many to muster. Neither of us has moved. Rex is still staring into the garden. It's as if an airbag has inflated between us to absorb the shock of the impact.

We have become instant strangers. Our intimacy, painstakingly laid down over thirty years, has been critically breached and I feel my life being sucked out the gaping hole.

I have to do something, so I take the dog for a walk.

Rex and I raise guide-dog puppies. Or should I say, we did? How soon do I start to frame everything in the past tense? Has that shift already occurred with the dropping of the A-bomb?

On our honeymoon in Bali twenty-five years earlier it was a different story. Like most newlyweds we were loved-up and full of the optimism that comes with being on the brink of a new life. One night we wandered in to a small local warung for dinner and, over a bintang and a dish of nasi goreng, we established that neither of us had that drive, hardwired into most people, to be parents. Not yet at least. We were enjoying this taste of travel too much. So, we made a pact. Instead of kids, we'd pursue a life of hard work, rewarded by exploration and adventure. We'd immerse ourselves in different cultures, push our physical limits in wild places, gorge on history and wine in the world's oldest civilisations. There was a synergy to our passions and dreams back then that made us feel inseparable and invincible. But we did agree that if either of us changed our mind about children, it would be raised and reconsidered. Now, our trainee puppies are our kids and they have brought joy, weighty responsibility and untold havoc to our lives. Heather is our second full-time charge. Amelie, our first, ended up dux of her litter and got a prestigious posting to Japan. Taking on that commitment and bringing her home at eight weeks, in a size 0 baby singlet, was as close as Rex and I got to parenting, and it bonded us anew in a way that was unexpected and enlightening all at once. We were in our fifties then and the shared responsibility of caring for a 'newborn' brought us closer as we fed, fretted, cleaned up messes and laughed while our furniture and shoes were chewed to bits. Right now, Heather is looking at me with those deep knowing eyes that dogs have when they sense something is wrong in human land. Guide dogs are bred smart.

I leave Rex fused to his chair and walk out to the back shed, careful to step on the bluestone blocks rather than the new turf. I find Heather's coat and lead, put them on as she squirms with excitement, then I press the remote to open the back gate and take her for a long walk around the familiar streets and parks of South Melbourne. She knows where she is going. I don't have a clue.

Nothing registers for me, except the script of the horror show replaying over and over in my head. Rex and Anna. Anna and Rex. In love. In cahoots. In bed together. Plotting, planning, discussing what to do with the old wife past her use-by date.

I am immersed deep in my misery when some strangers stop me on the street. My first thought is, oh no, please not today, not now. Everyone always wants to talk about the adorable little labrador in the blue coat and normally I am happy to oblige. So, I am surprised and off-guard when the older lady says directly to me, 'Sorry to interrupt, but I love your hair. Do you mind me asking where you have it done?'

Then her daughter says, 'And I really like your top.'

At which point I burst into tears, totally flummoxing both of them.

'That's nice to hear,' I say, 'but my husband of twenty-five years has just told me he loves someone else.'

These two strangers hug me and the younger one says, 'Well he's an idiot. Talk to your mum.'

'I don't have a mum,' I say.

'Well, you're welcome to borrow mine!'

Which I do, and I weep on her shoulder for as long as it feels seemly to do so.

An hour and a half later, as Heather and I turn the corner into our back lane, she quickens her pace and pulls on the lead. In anticipation of food and her disgusting orange rubber bone—and Rex. All the things she loves.

I punch the code into our roller gate and she does her customary little dance, spinning in circles, jumping with all four paws off the ground at once. Home is a happy place for her. Less than three hours ago, it was for me too. Now it's a foreign country.

I am caught between an unbearable reality and a tempting possibility. The thought forms. I could suppress the crime, bury the evidence, pretend it didn't happen. Clean things up and move on. Like they do in *Midsomer Murders*. Hope that no one suspects. But then my anger flares anew and I know I can't do that. It never works in Midsomer and it won't work for me either. My dignity won't allow it and a barely audible inner voice is saying, 'Enough Jo, enough.'

Instead, I invent scenarios that could possibly save me, and us. Perhaps Anna could be sucked into a black hole, or get run over by a bus, or be murdered by her own husband for being unfaithful. Did I mention that she is also very much married? This is the most galling thing. She already has a perfectly nice husband at home, but she wants mine instead. I've met him and they are ideally suited. Mr and Mrs Born-to-Be-Bland. In fact, I'm reminded of a strange encounter at the market recently, where, upon recognising Heather, a man approached me. At first, I had no idea who he was, but he explained that he was Anna's husband. It was a stilted couple of minutes in which we made awkward conversation about the bowling club and puppy-raising and the weather. All the while I had the impression he wanted to say more, but I was keen to get home and get started on the risotto, so we parted company and I put it completely out of my mind, until now. Now I wonder if he had seen the signs that I had so clearly missed. His manner suggested as much. Anyway, Anna's created not one, but two trails of destruction for the redundant spouses to clean up. Or she will have, when he finds out.

If he finds out.

There is, of course, always the very real possibility that now it's out she'll get cold feet and decide she doesn't want a father for a partner after all. Oh, wouldn't that be sweet? Wouldn't that put me back in the box seat? Rex would come crawling back and I alone could decide his fate. Take him back or chop off his treacherous balls.

These thoughts are diverting and they provide fleeting relief, but in just a few moments, I have to walk through my back door, where I know Rex will be waiting. Rex, the wrecker.

Of course, it wasn't always so. And, to be fair, it wasn't always Rex.

Two years into our marriage it was me who had an affair. So I have no right to assume the high moral ground. Though the circumstances and the reasons for my infidelity were very different and the outcome of that conflict was a détente that kept Rex and me together for the next twenty-three years.

Against all my adolescent predictions I found I actually liked being married. There was something liberating about feeling you had found your 'one'. That you could stop looking, stop wondering and start planning what your life would look like as a couple. I even noted that I felt a small frisson of pride when Rex started to introduce me as 'his wife'. We began making plans immediately, and got away whenever we could for weekends hiking in the mountains or chasing the sun and the surf. Every Friday night I'd spread a picnic rug on the lounge-room floor and lay out the treats I'd bought at the market. Cheese, olives, prosciutto, prawns, terrine, cornichons, salad and a crusty baguette. There'd be wine of course and much good-humoured banter, before we'd settle in for foot rubs on the couch and a movie on TV. We were blissfully happy until without warning we weren't.

Almost overnight, Rex transformed from the gregarious goodtime guy I knew, into a dark and impenetrable presence that I shared a very small space with. I had no idea what had brought about this change, but in the space of two years, I barely recognised him as the man I married and he barely recognised my existence—as a partner, or as a person. We lived in an apartment of four small rooms, but even so Rex seemed to be doing his best to avoid running into me. We both worked long hours, went to bed at different times. As a sideline to his management role at a prestigious Melbourne school, he coached its senior footy team. His dedication to the task was no less than would be required if the team were seeking League promotion, with every available hour spent at after-school training, weekend matches or in endless strategy and selection meetings conducted by phone long into the night. This schoolboy team was the only thing that gave his life any meaning and him any joy, even our second anniversary was sacrificed to the boys. I had lost my way to even reach Rex and my role in his life felt redundant.

In my loneliness and confusion, I grew close to a man at work. We had shared lunches over which I opened up and he listened. He was officially separated from his wife and had two fairly young kids, who were clearly his top priority. There was a vulnerability and a woundedness about him that made him attractive. The expensive well-cut suits and Hugh Grant hair didn't detract. *Debonair* is a word that springs to mind. So, not my type at all. My natural attraction was more to the feral surfie kind with tanned skin, long salt-stiffened hair and skinny, muscular legs poking out of oversized boardies. He was thirteen years older than me, past fifty, which I considered old at the time, and which oddly made me feel safe. Safe to be myself and safe to not be in the consideration set as his next wife, which he joked about whenever he saw an attractive woman, none of whom, incidentally, looked anything like me. They were always immaculately coiffed, expensively dressed, walking confidently on high heels, whereas I was more 60s-slim, fresh-faced, boyish pixie cut and ballet flats. Think Catherine Deneuve versus Jean Seberg. Nevertheless, our conversations, usually accompanied by a bottle of something aged and luscious that he could afford and I could appreciate, were wide-ranging and far-reaching, beginning with the common ground of being alienated by our spouses, but meandering along paths that wasted hours in articulate diversion. Architecture, popular culture, Japan, what makes a great ad, philosophy, people and lots of politics. The talk was the start of my downfall. I recognised it as a missing mainstay of my marriage, especially in recent times, and I realised I was beginning to look forward to our time together a little too much. This man was there for me when my husband wasn't, and being in his company felt like walking into a warm cosy room full of comfy sofas where I was welcomed rather than shunned. For months our intimacy remained intellectual, but conversation is a mighty powerful aphrodisiac, and inevitably, with me able to overcome the age difference and with the verbal foreplay of minds meeting, it crossed the line. A kiss that had been a long time coming led to a coupling that deepened our bond and took us to a more dangerous place. It wasn't love exactly, but it was a connection that was becoming increasingly difficult to hide.

I decided I had to tell Rex and was waiting for the right time. But for news like this, there is no right time, and I really had no idea how he would react. We were essentially an estranged couple living under the same roof. He had provided ample opportunity for me to be absent without being missed, so he was not suspicious at all. We had drifted so far apart that I thought perhaps he might be relieved to be rid of the burden that was me.

Two years in, I didn't want a broken marriage, I didn't expect to be an unfaithful wife, and I didn't want to face his wrath. But I really didn't know what I wanted either. Not Rex in his current form. Not my recent lover on any long-term basis. All I knew for sure was that I had to get away, get some perspective and find out.

When the confession finally came, Rex was more hurt than I imagined he'd be and he lashed out at me personally. Whether because he still cared about us, or because his ego had taken an unexpected hit, I'm not sure, but his initial response was loaded with vitriol rather than regret.

He called me an accomplished liar; he told me I worshipped false gods (presumably because I worked in the dark arts of advertising); he accused me of being selfish and elitist and he said I had done nothing for him in the past two years. Were these admonishments deserved? Maybe, maybe not, but for an unfaithful wife there's not much recourse in these early moments, and in the face of that kind of censure I wasn't inclined to stick around and argue. The time would come for rational discussion, but it was not now.

I moved into the first affordable place I could find, a depressing one-bedroom apartment that reflected my state of mind. I thought things couldn't get much worse, but on my first weekend alone, I watched Anthony Green declare John Howard victorious over Paul Keating in the 1996 federal election. I looked on in disbelief as I saw a family direct from 50s central casting take to the stage, claim victory and in so doing compound my grief.

On top of that, the man who had been the catalyst for my current situation, told me he'd agreed to give it another go with his wife for the sake of his kids. I applauded that, but now I had lost Rex, I had lost Keating and I had lost my lover.

I had some serious soul-searching to do. And I'd landed myself in the perfect place to do it. A soulless prefab concrete box in St Kilda with absolutely no redeeming features. A cheap cell for my penance.

I am an inveterate list maker, intermittent diary keeper and constant note writer.

Under the heading 'What I would miss about Rex', I wrote:

- Summers and the soporific soundtrack of cricket commentary
- The vision we shared for a happy life
- Friendship and laughs (in short supply of recent times)
- Playing golf together
- Belonging
- Five o'clock films at arthouse cinemas, followed by dinner and movie dissection
- The prospect of dying without each other
- Travel, holidays and planning our next adventure
- Road trips, arguing over the music
- Reading and comparing notes on books
- Prawn and pork sui mai at Num Fong

Below that, I wrote:

> I am not desperately unhappy without him. I miss him, but I don't miss the anxiety that comes with him. And I don't know if we are right or good for each other. Too hard?

I spent many long hours alone weighing the pros and cons of our relationship. Where I was didn't feel right. Going back didn't feel right either. My thinking was infected with selfish and cowardly thoughts. Will anyone else ever want me again? Should I stick with the devil I know? Emotional bravery is not one of my strong suits, and the prospect of being alone in my forties filled me with a deep dread.

If only I'd known what was to come.

Rex was not letting go easily either. He sent me letters. They were not strictly declarative, but there was a sense that he wanted us to try again, and an implied sense that if I didn't come back soon, I would miss the boat.

In one letter he acknowledged that happiness should not prove as elusive for us as it had over the last twelve months. But the fact that we had endured was in itself an achievement. In another he declared that marrying me had been the best decision of his life. He ended that letter with: *If you were willing to meet, I would welcome that. If not, I will accept that and move on.*

Rex's parents, who I knew liked me and, more importantly, thought I was good for Rex, took me to dinner to tell me he'd started seeing someone else. They asked me to please try to reconcile, saying *they* didn't want to lose me.

Then about six weeks into our separation, Rex phoned to tell me he had great news.

'What's that?' I asked sceptically.

'I'm depressed. Clinically, chronically depressed.'

I wonder in what universe this could be construed as great news.

But of course, Rex was relieved because he had seen a therapist and his blackness had been given a name. His moods were the result of a chemical imbalance. He had been diagnosed with a mental illness and it could be treated.

Before I could even process what he'd just said, before I could formulate a response, he had fast-forwarded to a rosy future where we are back together and everything is forgiven. In his mind, it wasn't him behaving badly, it was the illness that caused his withdrawal and dictated his foul moods. I'm sure that was partly true, but it felt a bit too neat and simplistic to me and I didn't know enough back then to realise that this abnegation of fault, this inability to see or accept any personal responsibility, was a red flag I should have heeded more closely.

All it did was throw more confusion into the already impenetrable tangle of thoughts and emotions that beset my brain. Damn you, Rex. Now you've added the assumption of 'moral duty' into the mix. What kind of wife, who'd agreed to the 'for better or worse' clause in the marriage vows, wouldn't answer a clarion call like that for support? What kind of a person would I be if I said no?

The diagnosis explained a lot about Rex's detachment, but it didn't really solve anything. I did some reading and learned that there were drugs available that meant it could be managed, but how effectively, I wondered, and at what cost in terms of side effects? And would those moods continue to visit like unwanted guests when we least expected them?

There was a song on the radio that I loved and it seemed to play incessantly. It was called 'Single' by Everything but the Girl. The chorus posed the question that swirled in my head over and over. Did I like being single? Did I want to go back? Tracey Thorn was singing my song, but she wasn't giving me any answers. Now I had this whole new thing to factor in. And if I was honest, I could do compassion, but 'carer' was not a natural role for me.

When I first moved out, I decided to take a break from the pill. I figured I wouldn't have much need for contraception and, in addition to a mental cleanse, I was ready for a chemical one as well.

Then one night soon after Rex told me about his diagnosis and after I'd met with his parents, he invited me to dinner at our apartment. He wanted to talk. And he'd made an effort. He served oysters and crayfish and made a really nice salad. He even produced a bottle of my favourite wine.

The conversation circled around the many topics that fed into whether we should give it another go or not: the talks he'd had with his psychiatrist; his prognosis for recovery and ongoing management; my affair and where we stood on that; our willingness to try and our fear of failure; our chances of being able to put this dark chapter behind us and re-establish trust. On that last point our track record was not good. We had only been married for two years, though we'd been together on and off for seven. That included a massive pre-marriage split occasioned by Rex soon after we'd bought our first house together. More on that later. But still, it was early days in our relationship.

We ate. We drank too much. We arrived at no resolution. But it was too late and I was too drunk to drive home, so we ended up in our marriage bed. When he undressed, I saw that he had bruises all over his neck and chest and my first thought was that he had been in a fight. Then I saw them for what they were, love bites, and I wondered if that was the purpose of the whole exercise—to make me jealous. To show me that if I didn't want him, there was someone else who did.

After more accusations and recriminations, me calling him a pathetic, arrested adolescent, him hurling my own deceit back at me, we fell asleep, and in the morning, had ugly, acquiescent sex.

And I got pregnant for the first and only time in my life.

I reflect now that this episode presented me with two life-changing sliding-door moments:

1. I could keep the baby.
2. I could leave Rex.

I chose neither.

Instead, with Rex's approval, I terminated the pregnancy, though it was not him but my good friend Eve who drove me to the clinic and helped me navigate the barrage of right-to-lifers blocking the doorway. I'd been clear about my decision not to go through with the pregnancy, but on the day, I was more than grateful for Eve's support, because I'd underestimated the effect of those protestors placarding outside, and also of the questions I faced once inside. The decision was more shaded than I'd imagined, and the nurse, simply doing her job, raised doubts I had not, until that moment, properly considered.

It was never going to be an easy reconciliation with Rex and the opportunity we had just surrendered added to my guilt. Our wariness of each other meant we were constantly on high alert, setting up trip-wires and ready to accuse. When we acknowledged we'd never make it work with that kind of distrust in play, we arrived at a completely pragmatic reckoning of events. We decided to call it 'one all', agreed to withhold the artillery fire and pledged never to let infidelity in the door again. And for twenty-three years, as far as I know, we didn't.

But going back to those sliding doors for a moment.

What if I had chosen to have the baby? How might that have changed our lives? Would we have been happier with another person to care for and worry about besides ourselves? Would a baby have brought us closer together, solidified us when the glue of reunification was still setting? Age-wise, the timing had been pretty perfect: me thirty-seven, Rex thirty-nine. But in terms of where we were, personally and as a couple, it seemed all wrong.

I felt uncomfortable that I had conceived in fraught circumstances and I feared irrationally that somehow those circumstances would leave a deep psychological impact on the baby. Then, there was always the very real possibility that we wouldn't make the marriage work.

Two years later—probably because my body clock was screaming 'It's now or never!' I did raise the issue with Rex, just as we'd promised we would. (Coincidentally, we were in Bali—where the original pact was made.) He was still of the opinion that our life was pretty good without kids and reminded me that we had travel plans and adventures we had yet to realise. I had trouble mounting a good argument against that and, because having a child now seemed more driven by my time running out than my desire to be a mum, we let it go.

To this day, though, I still think about how different things might have been. Would that baby have saved our marriage? Would we have made good parents? That child would be grown up now. What would he/she have been like as an adult? All those things I'll never know. I don't regret the decision, but I do still occasionally mourn the loss.

And what of the other sliding door? What if I had chosen to leave Rex? After I'd moved out, I'd felt I was on the cusp of becoming someone different. I was living alone for the first time in my adult life and had I been brave enough to sit with that for a little while longer, I may have learned important things about who I was. My self-awareness remained badly underdeveloped, largely due to my fear of being alone, but to undertake exploration of that kind required a leap of faith that I just wasn't brave enough to take. Faced with the choice of restarting a life plan that had stalled or jumping into the abyss, I chose the former: to put my faith in marriage and modern medicine, and instead of now being suddenly single at sixty, I could have been fearfully free at forty, and writing a whole different story.

As I walk back in the door with Heather, I realise I don't know who I am in this new reality. Still Rex's wife, but no longer his confidante. He is the person I know best in the world, but I can't ask his advice on this one. I want to hold him, I want us to comfort each other, but I also want to lash out and hit him. Many times over. Rex has removed his coat and scarf but is still welded to the chair I left him in, and on any other day at this time, we would discuss dinner plans. But we are no longer 'us'.

He says, 'You've been a long time, you must be hungry,' and he suggests going to the market together. Clearly, he too is struggling with the rules of realignment. We're in our familiar living room, Heather is lying at his feet, the sun has come out and a ray of light shines across her and our beautiful timber floor. Nothing has changed, and everything has changed. Our 'normal', imperfect as it may have been, has been napalmed.

As much as I want to suspend reality or even rewind time, I am compelled to tell someone, someone beyond the two strangers I met on the street, knowing that with the telling, it will become real and there'll be no stuffing the genie back in the bottle.

Eliza is my business partner of twenty years. Our relationship I think of now as my good marriage, the one that really worked. It began twenty-two years ago when, in my role as creative director at Adtown, I was desperate to find freelancers to help out over our busy Christmas period. The Myer Christmas catalogue had to be shot and I needed good fashion art directors I could trust to send to Sydney unsupervised. I'd heard about this gun for hire called Liz Woti and in the course of my fruitless search to track her down, I kept getting calls from a very persistent Eliza Wilsmere. Eventually, running out of time and options, I agreed that Eliza could bring in her folio. Turns out Eliza and Liz were one and the same person. Liz Woti was her married name and she was no longer married. I'm not sure if I was more impressed by her folio or by her. Her work was really good, full of smart ideas and brilliant executions, but it was her personality that shone. She vibrated with life, had a huge smile and a barely contained joie de vivre. I hired her on the spot.

Two years later, when Myer decided to change agencies and it looked like we'd both be out of a job, Eliza and I decided, with an abundance of naivety and an alarming dearth of business experience, to start our own thing.

'Working Girls', our very own ad agency, was born on

the eve of the new millennium and it lasted for a full twenty years. That's a lifetime in business terms and it's a long time in a partnership of any sort (truth be told I probably spent more time with Eliza—give or take—than I did with Rex, since I was with her five days a week, eight hours a day), but it worked because we balanced each other perfectly. She was the firecracker; I was the steadying force. She was the blue-sky thinker; I was the strategist. She could sell anything with her flamboyance and inspirational pictures; I could seal the deal with my rationales and heartfelt copy. If she rubbed people the wrong way, which she sometimes did, I'd smooth things over. If I got stuck or objectionable, which I sometimes did, she'd be right behind me pushing me through the mud.

Ours was a success based on chemistry, passion, skill, speed and timing. Faced with a new or tricky brief, we'd take ourselves offsite, normally to her place, make a pot of tea, get out the butcher's paper and black markers, and within a couple of hours have about five decent ideas, three of which we'd fine-tune, dress up and present back to the client, almost always hitting the mark with one or more of them. We amassed a small but extremely loyal group of core clients, who kept the business profitable, while others popped in and out over the duration to keep things interesting. At our height we employed sixteen people. Our legacy— unintended but extremely gratifying—was that we were trailblazers for women in advertising and Melbourne's first all-female-run ad agency. We made up our own rules, which attracted a bunch of like-minded women who loved our flexible work practices and generous concessions to motherhood. When Eliza wanted to have a baby, she took three months leave, with the understanding that 'travel' was my baby and I'd take my 'maternity leave' in Europe, thanks very much. That's how Rex and I managed our first extended break.

Of course, there were difficult times, the worst being when clients left us and precious people had to be let go. That was never easy, and due to my chronic inability to deal with conflict, it would normally fall to Eliza. Then there was the time we somehow managed to run the wrong ad in the *Age* three weeks in a row, for an important client. That was costly and strained relationships to breaking point, but we pulled through and there was seldom a day when I didn't look forward to getting into the office, making a cuppa and doing the morning 'around the grounds' with Eliza and the team. Before the real work got underway, we'd recap the latest ep of *Married at First Sight*, discuss who was leading in the footy tipping comp, relive last night's dinners, catch up on the dating status of the youngsters and generally solve the problems of the world.

Way back when the notion of going into business together first formed, we ran it past a mutual friend and mentor telling him we wanted to be like Melanie Griffith in the movie *Working Girl*. In his droll and understated way, he said 'Great, go with it, and by the way that's your name—Working Girls.' Then we were advised by an accountant that to be legit, we'd need to set up a business bank account. We had no cash at the ready, so to create a starting balance we each had to borrow $5000, and before a bank would lend us that kind of money, it required a 'Business Plan'.

A *what?*

This was what we came up with:

> Do good work. Work with good people. Have a life outside of work.

Not really what the bank meant by business plan, but it lent us the money anyway.

I'm proud to say we stayed true to that plan for the duration of our days in business, and we often shared it with clients who found the simplicity and truth of it refreshing. It won us a lot of hearts and minds and persuaded quite a few clients to ditch the big guys with the flash cars and go with the smart girls and the sassy attitude.

So, as I sift through the options of who'll be the first to know about my news, I settle on Eliza. Her resumé of life experience qualifies her admirably for the job. Together, we have been through the death of her mum, her marriage, the birth of her son, bouts of depression, her divorce, various subsequent partners. I have been her rock, the stable one. Now it's her turn to dish out the tough love and sympathy.

Turns out she's very good at it. It seems her time in therapy has paid off.

I pick up my phone and Rex asks what I am doing. I say I am going to call Eliza and go to her place. Without missing a beat, he says, 'Do you mind waiting until I tell Anna? We had an agreement'—*they had an agreement*—'that if this came out, I'd tell her before anyone else.'

So, there it is. I now have no doubt where I stand in this new reality. It has just been made brutally clear by the audacity of that request. Rex, who I have loved and looked after for thirty years, prioritises his mistress's feelings above mine. I cannot believe that their 'agreement', shaped somewhere in the limerence of the last five months (if the time line is to be believed), is more important than my welfare in this watershed moment.

That is the line—finally I am incensed. Fury flares like a blowtorch and, with just enough presence of mind to safeguard my phone, I grab the next nearest thing, which happens to be a half-full cup of cold tea, and hurl it at the stranger who just said that. He ducks and it smashes against the fresh white wall, staining it with streaks of black tea. Stained like my marriage. Rex looks suitably cowed by my outburst and quickly puts his phone down. For now, Anna will have to wait.

I move to the dining room, pull the sliding door closed behind me and have what is the first of many conversations I don't want to have and barely have the words for.

When she answers the phone, Eliza is driving her son to school camp and I realise I'm on speakerphone. 'G'day, Beryl,' she answers with jovial familiarity, using the name she calls me at work. But then she hears my voice. Today I am not Beryl to her Agnes. Our comic workplace personas have no place in this conversation and she knows I'm not ringing to ask if she wants her afternoon cup of tea, for which those names were first coined. 'Cuppa tea, Bez?' 'Love one, Ag.' Hearing my shaky first words, she anticipates an eruption that is about to fill her car with emotional debris and shuts me down—fast—protecting Rory from a conversation he's too young to hear. Let him abide in youthful innocence a little longer. I am relieved when Eliza tells me to go to her place and wait for her there.

She is still a long way from home when I arrive, so I locate the hidden key and let myself in. Her dog (tragically also called Rex) bounds up to the door and becomes the perfect companion, unlike his namesake. I tell him everything. I wet his fur with tears, I stroke and kiss him and almost suffocate him with grief and love, and he doesn't flinch. In fact, he looks up at me baring his cute little overbite and seems to ask for more. I think of Heather at home and immediately put the thought out of my head.

When Eliza finally appears about two hours later, I am sitting in front of the TV, drinking wine, letting the flickering images wash over me, not seeing or hearing anything. Not even registering that my beloved Pies are copping a hiding. She sits beside me on the couch and takes my hand. That simple human kindness undoes me, and in sentences broken by grief and disbelief and the need to inhale between sobs, I tell her as much as I know, focusing on the bit that bites hardest for me in these first horrific hours: I have been dumped for a younger woman. The unthinkable has happened 'to us'. How I believed it was unthinkable I will later come to question. I will understand that no one is beyond temptation and no relationship is ever impervious, no matter how secure it feels or what promises have been made, or how far through the darkness you have come. Still, right now I am having trouble accepting the fact that I am a sixty-year-old woman sitting on Eliza's couch and I am suddenly, tragically single.

While Eliza heats up chicken soup and toasts bread, I hover on the other side of the bench, watching and listening and hoping that she can make everything make sense. She is doing her best. She is the friend I need right now, compassionate, but there's no trying to gild the lily.

She avoids discussion of Rex, refusing to indulge my desire to crucify the bastard. Instead she patiently tells me that I will get over it. That I will have to find a way forward—if for no other reason than for her sake, for the sake of our business. Bless her. I can see what she's doing. She's trying to give me purpose when she can see that mine has been totally eviscerated. What she doesn't know, what she can't see, is that a force field has sprung up around me.

I'm encased in a titanium shield of victimhood; I'm light years away from any sense of purpose. 'Right now,' Eliza says, 'you're in shock and it's only five hours old, but in the morning, it will be twelve hours old.' My mind rejects this line of reasoning too. I am not ready to hear about time and its so-called healing properties. Right now, I can't even contemplate getting through the first night.

Eventually, she tucks me in to Rory's single bed, with Rex (the dog) for company. His tiny terrier weight is a comfort at my feet, but his snores and snuffles just remind me that I am not sleeping with Rex the man, the man I want to hate, the man who has landed me here in this single bed on the other side of town. But of course my contrary mind rewinds to happier times, to what I have lost.

When Rex was on top of his depression, he was amazing company, exuding an optimism that would infect all in his orbit. A powerful motivator, a patient teacher and a positive reinforcer.

He could get me to do things I would otherwise have been too scared to try, or felt incapable of mastering. He gave me self-belief and bolstered it with enthusiastic encouragement. He was trained as a PE teacher and he had a knack for lighting a spark in reluctant or fearful students. They listened when he assured them 'the head will say no, long before the body is ready to quit. If you can ignore your brain, your body will amaze you. Trust me.'

In his youth, Rex was a gifted sportsman, playing footy

and cricket at a fairly elite level. But as he aged, his joints made him pay dearly for that prowess with pain, surgeries and a truckload of prescription meds. At fifty, when his knees no longer allowed him to run, he started road riding, which I thought was completely insane and downright dangerous. Whenever he went out cycling, I always wondered who would later greet me at the door: him, or a couple of police officers to tell me he'd been hit by a car and killed.

Against the backdrop of that anxiety, he got me on a ten-speed bike and had me cycling in cleats. He got me descending safely at speed. He got me addicted to the thrill and sensation of freedom that a bike brings, and eventually he got me to the top of two of the most famous climbs in the Tour de France: L'Alpe D'Huez and Mont Ventoux.

Not in a group. Not supported. Just us, together on our own personal adventure—our joint achievement. It was part of a three-month bike tour of Europe (my 'maternity' leave) that was one of the highlights of our married life. We went to Spain, Italy, France and Corsica and concentrated all our favourite things: wild places, days spent pushing ourselves and our bikes to ever greater accomplishments, and nights spent recapping and rewarding ourselves with truckloads of food and wine that we felt we'd truly earned.

At the end of our extended trips, we established a tradition we called 'The Quiz'. It was like a recap and rating of our most recent adventure. We'd develop a set of questions together and then fill out our forms separately and compare answers. Things like favourite country, best town, best people we met, best hotel, worst hotel, best bed, best thing packed, best meal, best wine, best day of the whole trip and so on.

As it turned out, after that particular cycling trip, we had both nominated Mont Ventoux as our best day of the whole three months. I know I shouldn't do it, put myself through the agony, but in the tote bag I grabbed before I left home I keep a couple of diaries and I know the Ventoux one is in there. I switch on the bedside light, flip through the pages and find our entry for that day:

May 19, 2006, France
We wake to a beautiful, cool, bright morning and amazingly both have the same thought.

Let's take on the Challenge of Mont Ventoux. Let's conquer the Beast of Provence.

After a nervous breakfast and our host Claude warning us we are 'fou' (mad), we drive to the town of Sault which will be the launch pad for our climb.

We unpack our bikes, and set off in bright warm sunshine, having run out of all possible excuses not to ride. We try to warm up our legs by spinning furiously and gradually the nerves settle as we start to enjoy the rhythm of the climb.

At the 18-km marker we both feel fresh and optimistic about our chances of reaching the summit and set off for the last push with high hopes. Little did we know that the Beast that is Ventoux was lying in wait for us, licking his lips. All is still well when we reach Le Chalet Reynard which marks only 7 kms to go—until we round a bend and see what lays in wait. The mountain is now completely bald and the two towers at the top look tantalisingly close. It's only when your eyes take into account the size of the cars and the cyclists above that you understand the perspective and the enormity of the task. They are like tiny ants, moving ever so slowly (or not at all) as they fight the massive headwind roaring down each gully.

One kilometre from the top the wind defeats me and I pull over at the famous Tommy Simpson memorial. I look up to the summit to see Rex has made it. He sees me, waves and indicates I should stay put.

He rides back to me very tentatively because the wind is now dangerously strong, but I hold my nerve on the upper reaches of the exposed mountain and soon we are back in the forest and the descent is truly amazing. Fast and smooth and seemingly endless. The kilometre markers speed by and before we know it, we are grinding up the short steep climb from the floor of the valley to Sault. Tired but triumphant, we pack up our bikes and drive home to St Saturnin.

What to do after such a day?—the best restaurant in town of course. We settle on L'Hotel du Voyageur and choose the 30-euro menu. Beautiful food and fine service provide a fitting end to a truly remarkable day.

I recall now the toast Rex raised to me at the start of that night: 'Well done, Tommy,' he said. 'I'm so proud of you.' And Tommy remained my nickname for the rest of the trip.

I close the diary, my eyes burning with salty tears, eyelids swollen like ant-bitten body parts. How can I give up a future filled with more days like that? How can he? And why now, when we're on the cusp of creating so many more memories just like that one?

I keep circling back to the unfairness of it all. We've worked hard all our lives on our marriage, our health, our nest egg, our priorities—all geared to this point in time. And instead, vanilla little Anna slinks in and robs me of my reward, my retirement dream and my life partner. The cruelty of the timing is the worst. It threatens to burst me apart, making me feel murderously vengeful and pathetically forsaken.

Finally, I see light at the window. Somehow, I have made it through the darkest night of my life, but sleep has not played its restorative role and I seriously don't want to face the day.

It's Sunday of the long weekend and tonight Rex and I have tickets to see *The Book of Mormon* with our good friends

Justin and Fiona. Now I have to let them know I may be coming on my own, or not coming at all. So, of course I take the easy option and text. How do I start to tell people, my friends and my family, that my marriage is over? That Rex has traded me in for a fresher, younger model. That he has done what we have so often pitied others for, smug in our assumed contentment. Rex and I were good together. Or at least I thought we were.

Justin is a judge. A good one. A fair one. A real-life, bona fide wig-wearing one. I've known him since high-school days, when we were both country kids growing up in the Yarra Valley, and we have remained friends all that time. He calls as soon as he receives my text and invites me over to their place for breakfast. He warns me that he is in his Cats pyjamas (he is a diehard Geelong supporter). I assure him that, however bad he looks, I look worse. I am unmoored, unslept, on remote control, so I just do what I am told and head to their place in Carlton.

When they open their door, both Justin and Fiona have looks on their faces that I can't readily interpret. They are sympathetic for the state I am in and they console me with big heartfelt hugs. But even through my emotional fog, I sense something lurking behind those hugs that's unexpected. I sense anger. Not at me, but for me. I sense knives ready to strike. I sense an inevitability. Something is about to be revealed.

Turns out I'm right. Sitting on their couch, being plied

with perfect push-button coffee, I learn that Rex and my relationship has often been a 'topic of concern' within our circle of friends. That people talk about the way I am treated, and wonder why I put up with it. That for too long they and others have witnessed Rex's bullying and stayed silent. That they too have capitulated to Rex simply to keep the peace. Justin talks of a holiday we shared in France where Rex insisted on a cycling route that was beyond most people's capabilities. When the riders started to fall like flies and call for back-up, Justin regretted not speaking up. There is no joy in the telling, no suggestion that I should have known better, no portrayal of me as the patsy. But there is a clear and imperative sense that I need to listen. I sense their discomfort with the weight of the task they have taken on, but I acknowledge their courage.

The most telling thing for me is that they are not at all shocked that I am here. Seems everyone saw it coming but me. Suddenly, my personal distress is compounded by this very public humiliation. Of course, on some level, I am conscious of my abasement—of the concessions I make in the name of harmony—but the shameful revelation is that other people see it too. I thought it was my guilty secret, so secret I barely saw it. I actually thought our public face and life were ideal. The stuff of envy even. Lovely terrace home in South Melbourne, amazing holidays in Australia and overseas, rewarding careers, wonderful friends. I even thought we were solid enough to get to the 'until death do we part' bit.

Now I learn that, in some quarters, our breakup will be viewed as good news.

This is hard to hear. I have loved Rex...maybe still love Rex. Certainly not enough time has elapsed for me to 'unlove' him. I'm not sure I want to go on without him—can go on without him. We stuck by the Bali pact to remain childless and pursue a life of hard work and reward, and, up until now, we've fulfilled that promise. At our best it's made for deliriously good times and indelible memories, at our worst, challenging times that have tested us both, but, bottom line, we have been there with and for each other. Until now, I would have called that reliance mutual. But for Rex it seems the rope of reliance is fatally frayed. For me, I'm hanging on to that rope—to hope—for dear life.

I leave Justin and Fiona with them willing me to stay strong. They've made it pretty clear they don't think Rex deserves any more chances, but I know they are afraid I will revert to type. Justin's parting words were, 'No back-pedalling, Jo.' But what they don't get is that to stay strong, you first have to *be* strong, and I am far from that. I am broken and sick with dread for the two things I have to do next. First, I have to phone our best friends Eve and Martin and tell them what has happened. Normally I would have told them first, but I chose Eliza because I knew their threshold for bad news was already stretched to the limit with the recent death of a close friend, the ongoing health concerns of Eve's mum and the antics of their son whose ability to find trouble was continually reaching new heights.

In my car, driving down Punt Road with traffic swirling all around me I know I pose a bigger threat than any drink driver. My mind is everywhere but where it should be, that's confirmed when I attempt to change lanes and almost side-swipe a brand-new BMW. Only his last-minute horn saves his shiny black duco from the panel shop. He gestures to me in his rear-view mirror, 'What the fuck?' To him I'm just some crazy old lady who shouldn't be allowed behind the wheel and to me he's just part of the problem—men who think they are invincible and entitled.

Even though my heart is racing from the near miss, part of me wishes I had hit him. When I cross the Swan Street bridge I turn left and pull over beside the Yarra to collect myself. I watch the slow flow of the brown river, the burqa-wearing barbequers on the banks, the kids on bikes and the steady stream of weekend runners lapping the Tan. I love Melbourne for its unique familiarity, its reassuring greens and solid greys, its resistance to flashy gestures and frivolous people, but I can't help resenting those runners with their shiny youth and carefree strides, whose biggest worry, I resentfully imagine, must be which pub to go to later to toast their saintly dedication to fitness. Rex and I used to do that too.

Should I call Eve or Martin? Eve, the friend I met at Monash University in the late 70s while we were both studying to be teachers. She was a tall striking blonde, a first-generation Scot, with a high ponytail that ended halfway down her back, clear blue eyes, full lips that were always perfectly lipsticked in a brilliant shade of red that never came off no matter how much she ate or drank or kissed, and outrageous costume jewellery that put her firmly in the fashion-forward zone. She would always rush into lectures at the last minute and sit by herself in the front row. You couldn't miss her. I thought she was fascinating and just a little bit scary, so I was totally gobsmacked when the queen of cool asked me to be her partner in a duo production requested by our drama tutor. Things got better still when she suggested we do our lesson plans at the Nott, the uni watering hole, later progressing to prac prep in her tiny backyard in Prahran, where she'd produce a cask of wine and a platter of cheese and we'd do the minimum work, but sow the seeds for a lifelong friendship. It was there too that I met Martin, who I learned was her second husband, and her five-year-old son Daniel, from her first marriage. Turns out the reason she was always late for lectures was not, as I thought, because she wanted to make a grand entrance, but because her babysitter would be running late.

Eve picks up on the second ring and I ask if Martin is there. I tell them to sit down and put me on speakerphone. I have some news.

'Is it Rex? Is he okay?' With his track record they immediately think he's had an accident, or worse.

'Yes, he's okay,' I say, 'but I'm not so good. He told me he's in love with someone else.'

I hear the double intake of breath and the loud chorus of 'fuck' on the outtake. Before I can go on, they say, 'Come here. Stay with us. Stay for as long as you like.' I protest that they already have enough on their plate. That I'd already used up all the free board and sympathy I had coming from them on this score, last time I arrived dumped by Rex.

That was thirty years ago. Rex and I were not married then, but we had bought our first house together, which to my way of thinking was a much bigger commitment. It required more paperwork than marriage, and necessitated a large loan that we would have to pay off together. It was a bricks-and-mortar commitment, more solid I thought than some outmoded ceremony. But apparently not. In less than two years, the house was on the market. It was the late 80s, interest rates were at an all-time high and our relationship was at an all-time low.

But today my protest is lame and Eve and Martin's insistence, which I'm so relieved to hear, is steadfast, because I really have nowhere else to go and there's nowhere I'd rather be than in their familiar warmth.

No delaying any longer. Even with the immediate problem solved of where I will sleep tonight, I still have the second task to face: I have to go home (which will never feel like home again) and collect the stuff required for daily life: clothes, shoes, cosmetics, toiletries, medications, my Kindle, my computer, my heat pack, my hair dryer. I'd left in such a rush yesterday that I'd packed little more than a toothbrush. The thought exhausts me, not to mention the confrontation that lies in wait. I am overwhelmed by a deep fatigue that stops me from turning the car key in the ignition. Not just a lack of sleep, but a bone-aching, soul-enervating tiredness that tells me I don't have the energy for another breakup. And, besides, aren't I too old for this?

I recline my seat, close my eyes, let the afternoon sun warm me and let my mind wander.

It takes me back to Healesville, the small country town where I grew up, famous now as a wine-and-food destination, but back then known for nothing more than its wildlife sanctuary, extremely cold winters and a dearth of excitement. The main diversion for girls was boys, and for boys, cars. If the girl managed to get past the car to the boy, she would probably end up in the back seat, then pregnant, married and delusionally happy. That was not the future I wanted.

I am fourteen, sitting on a post-and-rail fence with my best friend, Hut, looking out over the paddocks of cows and sheep that held dominion here before the vines moved in. We are discussing the future, and I can remember distinctly saying to her that I would never get married, that the whole white-dress fantasy, so beloved of most girls, made me want to puke. We were listening to Led Zeppelin, *Slade*

Alive, Deep Purple and *Tubular Bells*; there was a whiff of marijuana in the air; and the world seemed potent with so much possibility.

At the end of high school, we both scraped through with very mediocre HSC scores that were good enough—just—to get us into Arts at Monash University. Thanks to Gough, our tuition was free and our world expanded.

So how did I end up here, in this car beside the Yarra, at sixty years of age, with a broken marriage I didn't want in the first place? Why did my lofty ideals crumble and give way to a tradition I'd been cynical about since I was a teenager? One day, about two years into our relationship, when Rex and I were visiting our friends Genevieve and Sven at their place in Shoreham, we saw a very cool modern house up for sale. We both loved the low-slung flat-roof style and it lodged in our minds. We talked about it all the way home, and again over dinner that night, finding a host of reasons to justify the infatuation that had taken hold of our senses. It was at the beach we reasoned, and we both loved the beach, it was a fairly easy commute to the city, so I could keep my job in Hawthorn, it was close to our good friends Gen and Sven, and best of all it was sort of affordable, whereas Melbourne definitely wasn't. Here was my longed-for commitment, not the frilly one I was adamant I would avoid, but a more solid one that would cement our partnership. We agreed to pool our resources and buy the house together.

Soon after we moved in, Rex landed a teaching job just up the road at Hastings High School, so it seemed the cards were well and truly falling in our favour. Meanwhile, I was still doing the hour-plus commute to Melbourne for work which meant I left early in the morning and usually got home after dark. It was a grind and soon got pretty tiring. To break the monotony of the travel, I'd spend one night a week in the small rented flat in Melbourne which I had decided to keep till the lease ran out.

That allowed way too much free time for Rex to kill. And kill he did, embarking on an affair with a fellow teacher who extraordinarily had the same surname as me. Someone joked that perhaps he was at a party one night and said, 'Come on Pecky, let's go home,' and left with the wrong one. I can laugh about this now, but at the time there was no funny side.

Fourteen months later our house was back on the market and my ideal of a committed relationship without a marriage certificate was in tatters. Even so, I wasn't about to give up on Rex. I moved back to my small flat in St Kilda and he stayed in the Shoreham house while it stubbornly refused to sell, our meagre salaries being eaten up by the seventeen per cent interest we were now paying, because of the 'recession we had to have'. The next few months were torturous, devolving into a toxic circular relationship that none of us could end. He kept seeing her, I kept seeing him and we were all miserable. He'd tell me that as he drove towards the city, towards us, putting miles between them, he physically felt her pull weaken and mine grow stronger, but that the same happened in reverse as he drove back to Shoreham, towards her. Finally, I went to a counsellor who gave me two solid pieces of advice. The first was: in any dysfunctional relationship, you get as much as you are prepared to put up with. Nothing will change until you raise your hand and say 'enough'. The second was: if you make an ultimatum, be sure you're prepared to carry it out.

My breaking point was reached when I came home early from a work trip and found a note under Rex's windscreen. It was from 'Pecky' thanking him for a lovely time last night. At this point we'd moved into a new rental property in Carlisle St and he'd convinced me that he'd stopped seeing her, given me his word. But that word was worth nothing if I couldn't trust him to keep it, if at the first opportunity he'd revert to his old ways. I was beyond livid when he walked through the front door a few hours later, greeting him with an outrage that caught him completely off guard, shouting at him that he was a filthy fucking liar, shoving the note of proof into his chest and leaving without giving him a chance to defend the indefensible, through a slammed door, the same one through which he had obliviously just entered.

The next morning, a Friday, I gave him my ultimatum: marry me, or I buy the *Age* tomorrow, find a place of my own, and we're done. DONE.

To my amazement, I meant it. To my even greater amazement, he proposed on Saturday morning before I even had a chance to go to the newsagent. He produced flowers, he got down on one knee, he told me he wanted this and that he could, and would, be faithful.

We got married at the Melbourne Registry Office in April 1992 with Eve and Martin as our witnesses. I wore navy, my bridal car was Martin's delivery ute, and we disappointed most of our family and friends by 'cutting them out'. But my fourteen-year-old self would never have countenanced anything else. I still didn't want the wedding, but I did want the man. And if this was the only way I was going to keep him honest, I thought I could make that compromise.

Now as I think back, I wonder whether it was a great strategy. Had I somehow tricked Rex into marrying me before he was ready? And why did I want him so badly, after what we'd already been through? Did I simply, egotistically, need 'to win'? And was he ready to marry again, or was his behaviour a clear indicator that he was not, and maybe never would be? I knew he was having trouble getting over the failure of his first marriage, being a man who can't abide failure in others or himself. My dogged determination must have had some foundation though, because in spite of that inauspicious start, and the hurdles we negotiated over the course, we lasted twenty-five years. That's not insignificant.

Now, as I sit here beside the Yarra, I wonder, is it really over this time? Is he going to give me up for her? Am I going to let him? Could I stop him? Should I try? The answers are far from clear and, in these early hours, as fugitive as a mirage. Given the chance, would I want to reconcile? Rex is not always easy to love, but I've also found him very hard to leave. Usually, I've managed to paper over the cracks in our facade of domestic bliss, but maybe this time I'm a little too beaten and those cracks have opened a little too wide.

With the sun disappearing behind the trees, I raise my seat back up, turn the key and drive 'home', where Rex greets me at the front door with visible unease. I brush right past him, barely acknowledging he's there, because I have no idea what to say and also because I think any softness from him, any kind words or sorrys, will bring me undone, and I need steel. He follows me upstairs and into our bedroom where I have already grabbed a suitcase and started to fill it with clothes. He sits passively on the bed and watches me, saying nothing, which only infuriates me more. From the depths of my hurt I say, 'Could you at least not bring her here, not to our bed?' He shrugs his shoulders in a way that says, sorry, too late for that. Whether deliberately or not, his actions are making my resolve so much firmer. Then he cares, just enough, to ask me for the second time in two days where I am going.

'To Eve and Martin's.'

'That's good,' he says. 'I know they'll look after you.'

'They shouldn't have to,' I say. 'They have enough going on, as you know, but they are kind people and they are used to me showing up on their doorstep dumped by you.'

Then I shout at him to leave and let me pack in peace. And do you know what? He doesn't. He just sits there in silence and watches while I randomly pull pieces of my life and pile them in the case. I have no idea what is going through his head.

In the immediate aftermath, so many people asked, 'Why did you leave? Why didn't you kick him out? After all, the situation was of his making, so why shouldn't he be the inconvenienced one?' The reason I give most often, because it's true, is that I lurched into flight mode. I had no desire to stick around and fight for my rights—I wanted to get the hell out of there. My home suddenly felt sullied by the knowledge that she had been in it—she had sat on my sofa, drank my gin, even slept in my bed. There were Anna germs everywhere and there wasn't enough disinfectant in the world to make that place clean again.

But the deeper reason—which I don't openly admit to anyone, rarely even to myself—is that I was so conditioned to keeping the peace and manoeuvring around Rex's moods that I continued to do so instinctively. Anything to avoid upsetting him. Anything to avoid confrontation. It had become my default position and if I was to learn anything from this sorry business, I had to try to understand why.

I was twenty-seven when I met Rex. I was dating a friend of his. In fact, we were guests at Rex's first wedding, making bets, along with many of the other guests, on how long it would last. Our prescience, as it turned out, was well-founded, but secretly I may have hoped for failure rather than just predicted it. For, in truth, I liked Rex and I felt disappointed by the mistake I thought he was making.

Rex was a good-looking guy in that Aussie surf life saver, sandy, salty sort of way. He'd arrived in Australia along with his parents, older brother and sister in 1962 as Ten-pound Poms and had been disappointed not to end up in a tree house in Queensland, as his parents had promised, but in the Nissen huts in Port Melbourne, where he was picked on by the locals for his funny accent and where to his further disappointment no kangaroos bounded down the streets. Twenty-five years later, Aussie transformation complete, here he was, an athletic, outdoorsy, broadly accented PE teacher, marrying another good-looking PE teacher. But where most people just saw the charismatic jock, I could see the intelligence he almost deliberately tried to hide. He had duxed his final school year and was accepted into law, but chose teacher's college instead. Perhaps because he grew up in Frankston where he shone as a sportsman, developed skills as a street fighter, had his pick of any girl and built a solid reputation as a lad, his popularity was cemented, but his intellect was seldom tested. Time spent in his company away from that milieu revealed a more nuanced persona, one that I was eager to delve into. So, after two years, when his marriage was all but over, and I was no longer seeing his friend, I unashamedly set my sights on him.

When we started seeing each other, he was still having trouble finally relinquishing his first wife, and she was having trouble deciding if she wanted him back or not. They made three attempts to reconcile, the last of which included Rex making a trip to Queensland for the sole purpose of bringing her and her belongings back to Melbourne so they could try again. But when the return drive of 2000 kilometres was spent in almost complete silence, they finally called it quits.

I, on the other hand, hung in there, and we kept seeing each other on and off. The powers of persuasion I was honing as an advertising copywriter I brought to bear with full force on Rex. One day, I wrote a list of fifty-two ways in which we were suited, and presented it to him as 'a pack' of reasons to stay together. Things like: you love eating, I love cooking, Max (his rottweiler) needs a mother figure, neither of us can abide fools. He laughed, he loved it, he agreed with it, but still he could not commit to me, to us. I continued to 'sell myself' to him through gestures big and small. We drove to Byron Bay in my brand-new Mazda 323 and had the first of our fabulous holidays together, establishing our mutual love of sun, sand and surf. I made an effort to differentiate myself from Wife Number One by being undemanding, understanding, acquiescent and a whole lotta fun—already setting up the patterns of behaviour that would metastasise and become a malignant force through the course of our entire relationship. Love me, Rex. Please love me.

How did this happen? How did I fall so far, when I'd grown up in the hotbed years of feminism?

I remember watching the ABC news on TV with my mum when I was just eight years old. It was 1965, the start of the 'consciousness-raising decade', and seeing two gutsy women chaining themselves to a public bar in Brisbane, insisting they be granted the outrageous privilege of being able to have a drink alongside their husbands, brothers and fathers. 'Good thing it's not like that with your father and me,' my mother said. It was the 7 pm news, so this would be after they had come home from the Healesville Bowling Club where they often had happy-hour drinks together and where women were not just allowed, but welcomed. On this night my brother would have been assigned the task of looking after me while they were out, but there were often times too when I was taken to 'The Club' and dad would shout me a sars and play table tennis with me.

When the 'It's Time' campaign swept Gough Whitlam to power in 1972, I was fully politicised and would have been burning my bra alongside my sisters, if I wore one. The next year, I was at Monash Uni, mixing in circles of smart liberated people who remain friends to this day. We were galvanised by Germaine Greer's *The Female Eunuch* and revolutionised four years later by Anne Summers' *Damned Whores and God's Police*.

How, in light of that background, did I become so acquiescent? Why did I tiptoe around Rex's black moods and bad behaviour? Probably because these were the parameters he and I accepted when we entered into our relationship and those patterns established early, as far back as I can remember, as far back as that first holiday together, stayed with us for the long term. I was not blameless in the way things turned out. And I was not an unwitting participant in the establishment of our particular dynamic. I went along with it because it seemed to be the price I had to pay to ride the highs. With Rex, the bad times were bad, and I'd found a way to live with those, but the opposite was true too. The good times were really good and I was addicted to those.

As I struggle to accept what's happened, everyone has their own way of helping. Most offer kindness and support—caring words which I soak up like a sponge, caring gestures that extend tangible comfort—a pair of handknitted socks, a hand-sewn quilt with the label 'Jo's Sanctuary'. Many send messages of love and hope. I have kept them all, but one from a work friend finds a special place in my ravaged heart, and on my pinboard. It is a quote from Albert Camus: 'In the midst of winter, I found within me an invincible summer.'

Bring on summer, I say!

And from the delightfully crude and incisive Inga: 'I hope his dick gets gangrene and drops off', accompanied by a rudimentary pencil sketch.

Others offer practical help.

Sandra, our general manager at Working Girls, draws up a spreadsheet of things I need to do and calls it 'The Power File'. Things like change my PIN numbers, close our joint bank accounts, cancel all periodic payments, change my will (already?), find a good solicitor, get Rex out of the house.

Another friend, Francie, acts like a forensic pathologist, investigating the dark corners of the relationship, trying to pinpoint what went wrong. A long-time friend to Rex and me both, she is determined to be fair, unafraid to ask the hard questions and unafraid to speak her mind. Faced with the revelation of the delicate situation I am in, most people say the right thing, or the trite thing, but they seldom tackle the true thing. Not Francie.

In her efforts to understand—and to be balanced—she spent long hours with each of us. She listened, she counselled, she offered consolation and solace, she even took notes and read them back to me but, in the end, she just couldn't make sense of why two of her favourite people, who had seemed to her so well suited, were splitting up.

In the early days she would meet Rex in the Botanical Gardens where they would walk and talk, the awkwardness allayed somewhat by not having to eyeball each other directly. She relayed a conversation she'd had with him soon after the split:

'Rex, what were you thinking? Did you not see a red light?'

'I know it's a madness, Francie, but it felt beyond my power to control.'

'That's ridiculous, Rex. Everyone has a choice. Did you not think about the consequences?

She's thirty-four years old, you're almost double her age. Do you seriously see a future with her?'

'I don't know, Francie. I guess I don't really know her.'

'Yet you were willing to cast aside your whole life based on—on what exactly?'

'She makes me feel good, Francie. I feel happy with her and bleak when I leave her.'

I think Francie takes it harder than anyone. She was Rex's friend originally and she hasn't really seen his dark side. Before he became her buddy, he was her boss, and she valued him as a fair and forward-thinking manager, a compassionate work colleague, an inclusive and reliable friend, not to mention the architect of some of her most fun times on group riding holidays in Europe and at home.

She compares the news to being hit by a hundred semi-trailers. Even I don't take it that badly. Well, that's not strictly true, I do, but it's not the infidelity that brings me lowest. I could probably excuse a casual fuck, call it an aberration and move on. It's when I reflect on words like: 'She makes me feel good! I feel happy with her and bleak when I leave her,' the only possible conclusion I can draw is that he felt bleak when he was with me. That's when the mania of wondering where I went wrong and why he chose her sets in.

Not long after the A-bomb was dropped, Rex and I met for lunch, ostensibly to discuss practicalities, but it was far too early to establish anything solid and in truth I think we just wanted to see each other, to assess how the other one was coping. We went to an Italian cafe in a church near where we lived. As the waitress approached with our table settings, she said, 'Calamari to share and rocket salad, or do you need the menu today?' Then she said, 'I haven't seen you two for a while, have you been away?' Rather than open that can of worms in public, we just said, 'Yes.' When she left us alone, Rex asked me how I was. Looking at him, at what I saw as composure but which might equally have been guilt or even sympathy, I couldn't trust myself to answer. He sensed the precipice I was on, and while he was holding it together, he could see that I wasn't. His way of consoling me was to take my hand and say, 'Don't worry Jo, you'll be fine, you'll find someone else. You're a catch.'

I don't even think he registered the irony of that statement until I said, 'Not to you apparently, Rex.'

Then he said, 'I guess it would have been better for you if I'd been knocked off my bike on Beach Road and killed.'

I didn't even have to think about my answer. There's dignity in death, but there's no dignity in being dumped. People know how to deal with widowhood. They offer condolences and casseroles. They send cards and flowers. But 'dumped' is harder to navigate. There's pity, which I feel acutely and despise. And anger, which is satisfying but not really helpful. There's disbelief and scathing contempt. But in the end, I'm on my own with my feelings. And all the while Rex is out there, very much alive, so I can't even mourn him. I just have to find a way to unlove, uncouple and unravel.

Now, with the benefit of hindsight, I'd say the heart breaks harder when you are young, when your dreams are built on a scaffold that reaches sky high (or in our case, on a low-slung first home loaded with love and possibility), so that when it comes, the fall hurts because it's such a long way down. But after thirty years, it breaks deeper, because in accumulating those moments, hours, days, years and decades together, you've laid down so much shared history, you have so much invested in each other, that the layers go very deep. It's no simple thing to even find your way out, let alone walk away from a life portfolio of that magnitude.

The thing that saved me in those first weeks was that I didn't have to go it alone completely. With Eve and Martin offering me a lifeline, I found enough familiarity to feel that I was still me, albeit missing a vital part. With their generosity I was still located somewhere recognisable within the landscape of my life.

The hardest thing about being at their place, though, was that for all those years, we were four. Rex and Jo, Martin and Eve. We holidayed, hiked and rode together in Europe, Japan, Byron Bay, Thailand and Tasmania, and at home we ate together at least twice a week. We celebrated our milestones together, of which there were many: Eve and Martin were the witnesses and only guests at our wedding, we knew each other's families, we were family. Now we were three. Eve and Martin—and Jo.

Eve and Martin loved Rex in the way you love your best friends, you accept them warts and all. But from the front-row seats they'd occupied for thirty years, they had felt the tension in our relationship, observed the inequity, copped the brunt of Rex's petulant moods, developed the strategy, as had I, of waiting for it to blow over and for funny, entertaining Rex to reappear. Every Friday night we had a standing booking at a pizza place called Fratellino, a casual catch-up that was always loaded with banter, bullshit and laughs and usually done and dusted in an hour. One night I inadvertently aggravated Rex by scratching his head in the way our tabby cat does every morning. It set him off and he turned on me slamming my arm hard against the brick wall. We were all so shocked we were speechless, and Rex, realising what he had done, just got up and left the table. Quite some time passed where we asked each other, 'Where did that come from?' Then Rex reappeared, sat down and continued as if nothing had happened. It seemed even he couldn't explain his outburst, so instead of trying, he simply said nothing. We all said nothing. And that's how it often went: outburst, shame, silence, move on. Martin later berated himself for not calling it out. He said, 'There had often been times when he could have—should have—punched Rex in the face.' But as I've heard now from many different people, they didn't do anything or say anything lest it embarrass me or make matters worse. And me likewise.

Now at close quarters, living as a single woman with Eve and Martin, I had the chance to see what a properly functioning relationship looked like. It was awkward for me at first, I felt like the third wheel, like I was imposing on their intimacy and tried to level up by helping with chores, but mostly just getting in the way and upsetting the established rhythm of their domesticity, so beautifully calibrated. Eventually we all found our level and worked around each other's routines. They let me pay board; they let me cook on Saturday nights; we worked out our shower routines;

and they gave me some responsibilities, like taking out the recycling and watering the garden. Small things that to me counted for a lot, and before long they agreed that having a new dynamic in the household had given them both a bit of a fillip too.

Suddenly, unexpectedly, I am a fan of *The Voice*. Eve dishes up something delicious for dinner, Martin pours the wine, we take our places on the couch and together we cheer and jeer from the sidelines.

We are united in our dislike of Delta, and our love of Boy George. We actually download the app so we can vote. We are that invested. Who would have thought? Anything to prevent Lucy from winning. She is insufferable. Already so entitled and articulate at fifteen, and Seal's fawning is even worse. We love the two big fellas, Hoseah and King Judah equally, and it's hard to choose between them. Fasikih is good, but she'll make it with or without our help. She's what they call 'the complete package'. Watching her, I think, 'I used to be a package once—now I'm a crushed cardboard box, ready for recycling. Wonder what I'll be remade as?'

But it's not just *The Voice*, I am soon watching *Love Child, Janet King, The Unforgiven, Australian Ninja Warrior* and for a bit of high-brow, *Blue Eyes* (it has subtitles, so it must be classy). It's hard keeping track of so many different story lines, but on the upside, they're something to follow when my own narrative has stalled so spectacularly.

Eve and Martin have a small two-storey terrace in Prahran. The living areas are downstairs and the bedrooms upstairs. For me the levels are worlds apart. Being downstairs, in their company, watching TV, necessitates me keeping it together to interact and operate in a normal way, to help with the dishes and make the after-dinner cuppa, which I manage, all the while with a churning in my gut that never stops. My appetite has dwindled and I am losing weight that I don't really have to lose. But the routines of daily life and the discipline of adhering to them tethers me to reality, keeps me on the right side of functional.

It's a different story though as I climb the stairs to my bedroom. I feel the pretence of my being okay fall away with every step higher I go and as I shut the door to that room I surrender totally to my despair. That spare room at the top of the stairs became the place where I could indulge my self-pity without limit and where I would turn over and over the questions without answers. How could Rex so callously throw away thirty years of feelings, emotions, friendship? When had our happiness evaporated? Had it ever been solid? Why was I suddenly inadequate? Why her?

Rewind ten years. A decade before Rex dropped the A-bomb.

I was fifty and I was experiencing a whole different kind of hell. It was called menopause and I had the full catastrophe of symptoms: insomnia, mood swings, hot flushes, brain fog, teariness, anxiety and a general malaise with the world. I didn't realise what it was until I went to my doctor and she put a name to it. Such a relief to know I wasn't going slowly insane—although she did suggest I see a therapist.

Dr Barber—Terry—did the 'Are you depressed?' test and I passed with flying colours. Ten out of ten. So, to help me overcome the newly entrenched side-effects of my rapidly dwindling hormones, including depression, she prescribed treatment: chemical and psychological. I willingly took the drugs—anti-depressants and HRT—and relished the guided chats, and before too long I was able to resume a normal life and laugh again, so I have had faith in her ever since.

Not that I'd had any need to see her again. Until now.

'So, what brings you here, Jo?'

I tell her my sorry tale. I tell her I am a shell and I describe the emptiness that comes with that. I tell her I am furious because I feel I have been duped, not just for the duration of the affair, but possibly for the duration of the marriage. I tell her I am embarrassed. I consider myself a relatively sensible and intelligent woman. How did I not see what was happening to me? I tell her I feel cheated. Not because my husband fucked another girl, but because I have been robbed of my future. I tell her that I have excused behaviour from Rex that I would not bear witness to in any of my friends.

And then she starts to frame the questions and ideas that will shape our sessions and help me out of the mire:

'I want to hear about the power balance in your relationship. I want to know about your childhood. I want you to tell me what was good about your marriage. And what was bad. But right now, I want you to tell me where you think you stand. Do you want to save your marriage or do you want to move on?'

I think about this last question.

It's another of the ones that swirls endlessly for me day and night. I still don't have a clear answer and I don't know if Rex does either. But I try to respond to Terry from my own singular point of view. So, I tell her that the affair alone is not a deal-breaker for me. It's that coupled with the effort of keeping us buoyant, of trying to keep Rex happy, of waiting on the sidelines to be needed or wanted, I think I have reached my limit on that. Lately it has taken too much of a toll. I think I am done. I need to move on. Even as I say it, I feel defeated by the enormity of the task, by the effort it will take, and I seriously wonder if I am up to it.

On Terry's wall, there is a reproduction of *Christina's World* by Andrew Wyeth. It's not one of my favourite pictures, but Terry uses it to convey one of my most important lessons.

The painting shows a gentle country scene of a woman in a field. But if you look closer, you sense that something is wrong. Christina's position is not quite natural, not normal for someone sitting back and enjoying the landscape. She is, in fact, paralysed and ill.

Terry uses the painting to help me understand my inertia. To acknowledge that I too am hurt, wounded and fixed to the spot by the weight of my grief. And that although my injury is not visible like Christina's, it requires a similar force of will to overcome.

'Sometimes, Jo, we feel so disabled by the situation we find ourself in, that we are unable to move forward, terrified to look back. And we know that thinking only makes it worse. All we can do is switch to automatic and rely on action alone to propel us. Don't expect this to make you feel better or to ease your pain. The point is, Jo, you simply have to do something, anything, otherwise you'll go under.'

So, with no conscious volition, no desire to exist, no spark of joy, no future that I can grasp and a past that has been pulled like a rug from beneath my feet, I simply—do.

I *do* my hair. I put on make-up. I go to work. I walk because it is not far from Eve and Martin's place to my office and walking is *doing*. I tackle briefs with Eliza even though my creative edge is dull. I manage other people's problems, though I can't help thinking how petty they are compared to mine. I deal with clients, which is the hardest thing to *do* because it requires the biggest pretence. I *do* a day at the office and then I walk home. I *do* that on repeat five days a week, then it's the dreaded weekend. Eve and

Martin have a retail business so they are at work, Rex is with *her*, and without him as my partner in fun, I have no idea what to *do*.

Turns out I have a longstanding fear of abandonment, embedded at an early age by the untimely departure of my mother. I was eight when she developed cervical cancer and for two years I watched from the sidelines as she moved in and out of hospital and became less and less available to me.

In those pre-enlightened days, kids were pretty much kept in the dark about illness, especially terminal illness, so I never completely understood what was going on. I was seldom allowed to visit her during her long stay at Bethesda Hospital in Richmond, and when I did, I spent the whole time marvelling at how many get-well cards she had. I read them all and asked which was her favourite.

During the last months of her life, when, I realise now, that she must have been in palliative care in our local hospital, I didn't see her at all. Whether this was an attempt to protect me from seeing her so diminished, or simply a failure to see the importance of taking children on the journey, I don't know. But I distinctly remember the shock I felt on the day my dad took me out to the Hills hoist in our backyard in Healesville and told me that she wouldn't be coming home. I was ten years old. It was January and it was stinking hot. Our lemon tree was laden with fruit. I remember the mixed smells of the creosote-painted steps and Dad's sawdusty sweat as he tried to comfort me. I cried tears of anger and disbelief because I loved my mum more than anything in the world and I wanted her back. Although she'd been a shadowy figure in my life for two years, I was unprepared for this finality. For most of our short time together, we'd been an inseparable team.

I think she had enjoyed having a daughter at a time when she was better equipped for motherhood. And I was privileged to have her sole and undivided attention because my brothers, so much older than me, were already off doing their own things.

When she first became ill, I was angry with her because she was taking so long to get better. I was impatient to get back to the things we loved. When she was in bed, in pain, I'd be cross with her because she couldn't get up and come on one of our nature walks in the bush, where we'd fossick for moss, lichen and wildflowers. We couldn't make pumpkin scones together, or pick rhodies from the garden to arrange in vases. I couldn't swing on the clothesline while she hung out the clothes. Or wait while she hot-wired the old Ford Customline to take us down the street. One day when I was standing on the front seat—as you did in those days—she braked suddenly in the main street for a pedestrian, and I ended up on the floor under the dash. She put out her arm to stop me, but I catapulted over it. When she knew I was all right, we laughed long and hard about my acrobatic skills and a possible future in the circus.

I have a searing memory of another day when she caught her shin on the metal bumper bar of that rusty old Customline. Her cry of anguish in my six-year-old ears terrified me and my terror was exacerbated by the blood oozing thickly through her stocking; mums don't hurt themselves, I thought, mums don't cry. I was panic-stricken in the face of her distress, and more so to be rendered a helpless onlooker. All too soon the role of onlooker became permanent. I could only watch as each day she became more diminished by the cancer and so diverted by the pain that she withdrew from me. And with her went her love.

Terry suggests that this is where the rot set in. An unsuspecting and devoted child of ten loses her best friend. Absolutely nothing to be done about it, completely out of my control. But the lesson insinuates itself deep in the psyche. She points out that this would clearly have marked a devastating turning point in my life and so when it threatens to happen again, later in life, I'm hardwired by the memory of that loss to control what I can, regardless of the cost.

Which is why, over time, I put up with more and more from Rex and learned to accommodate our special brand of domestic derangement as the norm. The alternative, the possibility of being abandoned again, was just not an option for me.

In that respect I succumbed meekly and willingly to his

control, which was exerted in both big and small ways. 'I don't feel like talking.' 'I don't feel like walking.' 'I don't feel like watching a movie.' 'I don't want company tonight.' I got used to the dark cloud of dissatisfaction that hovered almost constantly above Rex, yet I could never pinpoint its genesis. Something I'd done was always my first thought, perhaps some personal issue I didn't know about, or more likely the depression that was constantly waiting to strike. I'd never know for certain because he'd never acknowledge its presence, let alone talk about it.

Our finances too were largely controlled by Rex. I was more than happy for him to manage the household expenses, but less happy about the way our discretionary spending seemed to be mostly at his discretion. With two road bikes and a mountain bike in the garage already he still 'needed' a fixie. Yet whenever I came home with a haircut or a new pair of shoes there would be an implied judgment that these were frivolous things 'we' could do without, or that surely, if I tried, I could source cheaper options. All despite me being the primary breadwinner.

Terry helped me to understand my complicity in this. In her view, by constantly swallowing my words and feelings, I had relinquished my rights in the marriage and abandoned my assertiveness for the sake of a 'happy life'. Me, who could be so strategically persuasive at work and so uncensored with my views in the wider world, would capitulate with barely a whimper at home. Of course, when I finally faced up to the truth of this, I was both astonished and ashamed. Clearly, in a balanced relationship I should have stuck up for myself, stood my ground. But even now, as an observer of my own history, I can't believe how compromised I became. And how passively I accepted my lot.

During the last twelve months of our marriage, Rex adopted wilful withholding as one of his major wrecking balls, but I even found a way of excusing that. He virtually stopped communicating with me. He made himself physically and emotionally unavailable. While I was still working full time, Rex, who had retired before me, would spend long hours at the bowling club 'practising', then when I got home at night, expecting not unreasonably some quality time together, he would be on the phone discussing teams, or club politics or the personalities who now seemed to dominate his life, like what to do without Jacko, who was their best player but was out on disciplinary charges for sexist and racist comments during the match at Elsternwick. When Rex was with me, he'd read the newspaper, but not discuss the issues of the day. Or do the crossword, but refuse to share a clue. We ceased to make plans. On one occasion, when I said I felt we had no shared life together anymore, he responded with, 'Get your own life then.' That stung, because it was proof positive of how far we had drifted. Still, I didn't snap.

Looking back, it was like he was being so obnoxious to me that it would be my decision to leave. He was waging a war of attrition, wearing me down slowly, so that if I did blink first and choose to go, he would get what he wanted: the freedom to run into the arms of his waiting lover with a clear conscience, without having to admit his guilt or accept any blame.

I've read since that's quite a common strategy for an adulterer and, if not for his depression, which I had learned to manage, and which I put this latest funk down to, it probably would have worked. Instead, I stuck the course, hoping all the while that we'd move beyond this particularly dark and entrenched episode, as we had before, and get back to making our plans for the future.

It was March and my sixtieth birthday was less than a month away.

Never one to celebrate a milestone, or crave the limelight, I'd managed to get through my first five decades, my twenty-first, even a wedding without ever hosting a big shebang. Probably because I'd always disliked being the centre of attention, and also because I wasn't a great lover of parties. My preference would always be a dinner with friends where you could eat, drink and talk, not only to the person next to you, but to the whole table and actually hear what they were saying. But as this particular milestone loomed, for some reason I felt differently. I wasn't afraid of the number, sixty didn't scare me and, damn it, I had reasons to celebrate. My life was in pretty good shape, Rex and I would soon be celebrating our twenty-fifth wedding anniversary, my business was ticking along and Eliza and I were making plans for my exit from the business at the end of the year. Compared to a lot of women my age, I was in pretty good shape physically too. Still fit and active, still the same weight I was at thirty and still able to turn a tradie's head, albeit from a reasonable distance. What I'd lost in facial elasticity, I'd gained in confidence and I was happy with the trade. So just this once I wanted my friends and family close, I wanted the speeches, I wanted the roasting and the reminiscing. I wanted to get dressed up, I wanted to dance and cut loose in the secure familiarity of my nearest and dearest, and I wanted it all to happen at the Albert Park Bowling Club.

Of course, Rex resisted. 'Let's just go away,' he said. 'Somewhere remote and exotic—an island,' he said. 'You hate parties,' he said. 'Let's have it at a restaurant where it will be less work,' he said.

'Anywhere but the bowling club', he said.

I never once twigged that his resistance was more ardent and even less explicable than usual. Of course, he had his reasons for not wanting it at the bowling club, but I was completely oblivious.

Finally, three weeks out from the date, he relented: 'Okay, have it your way.'

It wasn't much of an endorsement, but I didn't care.

Time was short, so I swung into action. First order of business was the food. It had to be good, my reputation rested on it, so I called the best caterer I knew, he agreed to do it and miraculously he was free that night. Together we selected menus that would accommodate every dietary obstacle and still taste amazing. It would be a sit-down dinner with shared plates on the table. Eliza and I designed a simple invitation and I sent them out before I could get cold feet. I went shopping for a new outfit and when I couldn't choose between two, I bought both, a tiered green silk dress from Alannah Hill that was way out of my comfort zone and a classic black dress from Saba that was more predictably me, determining to play it by mood on the day. I asked Eliza's son, Rory, to be DJ and to compile a list of gotta-get-out-of-your-seat songs, some oldies of mine and some newies of his choosing, with one stipulation: they had to have a good beat and you had to be able to dance to them.

On the day of the party our godson Jaran and his parents Remi and Frank arrived from the Blue Mountains. Remi was an ex art-director I'd met in advertising way back at the start of our careers. She had since transferred to the 'good side' and was now working as an aid worker for Childfund. I had enormous admiration for her, and was so proud when she and Frank asked Rex and I to be godparents to their adopted Thai son, Jaran. Not that God came into it in any way, Remi just wanted to be certain that if something happened to them, Jaran would not be abandoned for a second time. They were staying the weekend and I enlisted their help decorating the old clubhouse, stringing strands of colourful globes from the rafters, setting tables and agonising over where to place the name cards that Remi had so artfully handwritten. The combination of the old timber honour boards around the walls with their long lists of golden champions and the festive embellishment of the time-worn space pleased me greatly. It felt like the perfect reflection of who Rex and I were: sporty, unpretentious and welcoming, with an overlay of style that was mostly brought to the mix by me. I was a little annoyed that Rex had been unavailable to help, leaving it to this last minute to buy my present and card. He appeared briefly, wrote my card hastily at the bar and then went home to wrap the gift.

Even though I'd decided to put on a celebration, it was not going to be a big one. I'd limited the guest list to fifty people and forty-two had RSVPed with a yes, so the numbers felt manageable. That didn't stop me spiralling into a massive case of pre-party nerves and indulging my fears. Would those people from all different parts of my life, family and friends, get on? Would they mix? Would they be fidgeting and looking for excuses to leave as soon as the last course was served? By 4 pm I was feeling so anxious that, if I could have, I would have turned back time and agreed with Rex to abscond to Mauritius instead.

At home, which was only a short walk from the bowling

club, I tried on my two outfits. Rex preferred the black dress, so naturally that's the one I wore. I styled my short hair in seconds with my fingertips and a bit of product, applied some make-up in the way Eliza had taught me, eyeliner on the inside of the eye, a dusting of brown shadow, mascara and, because I refused to wear foundation ever, a light layer of tinted moisturiser, some highlighter on the cheeks, gloss on the lips, and I prepared to face the music, as it were. But as the guests started to arrive, my anxiety subsided. These were my peeps after all, here for me. I'd been to so many of their celebrations, but never returned the favour. It felt good to reciprocate at last, and the cosmos was playing its part too, turning on a beautiful warm April evening. The rink was open for barefoot bowling, the champagne and canapes were circulating and so were the guests, forming random teams and gladdening my heart with their easy laughter and chat.

Rex didn't want to make a speech, but had agreed to be master of ceremonies. Again, I was mildly annoyed as I watched him moving between the guests, hurriedly scrawling some notes before we moved inside. Evidently, he hadn't prepared, but he pulled it off, just, falling back on his charm and his ability to ad lib. In contrast, Genevieve and Eliza delivered fabulous speeches that were loaded with old stories and met with tears, from me, and big belly laughs from the crowd. Gen opened with, 'A while back I was travelling with Jo to Wycheproof in country Victoria for

Fiona's dad's funeral. I was waxing lyrical about the beauty of the quintessentially Australian landscape passing us by when Jo simply says "I hate fucking gumtrees!" That's our Jo, says it as she sees it,' Gen continued. 'Over twenty-five years we've watched Jo and Rex complement each other. The footy shorts and polyester shirts have disappeared from Rex's side of the wardrobe and in Jo's side there are now hiking boots, lycra and a well-used pair of golf shoes. Rex has undoubtedly encouraged the emergence of Active Jo. And she has steered the education of Cultured Rex. Over the years I have admired their respect for each other's work choices, their wonderful ability to holiday and travel in a *Gourmet Traveller* meets *Intrepid* style, and the time and love they have both put into nurturing their guide-dog puppies. Like most of you here, I have often enjoyed the generous hospitality at their house where there is always plenty of fabulous food and lots of guaranteed laughs.'

A generous and truthful summation of our marriage, but sanitised somewhat for the crowd and the occasion, given that Gen and Sven were close enough to also observe our cracks.

Then it was time for me to take the microphone. I am one of those people who rates public speaking right up there—above death—on the list of things to be feared most in life. Doing presentations to clients had made me a little more comfortable, but I was not a natural and addressing my peers seemed even more terrifying. Nevertheless, I had something I wanted to say, I'd thought about it a lot in the months leading up to my birthday, so I steeled myself and jumped in.

'At sixty, I have already been gifted twenty more years on this earth than my mum had. I look around this room and I see three cancer survivors. There are two people who should be here tonight, but can't be, and even if you think this is a shit party, I'm pretty sure they'd rather be here than where they are. So, if I hear any of you complaining about getting old, think about that for a minute. Old age is a privilege, and not one that can be taken for granted. So drink, eat, dance, kiss your loved ones and be grateful every morning when you wake up, even if your back is aching or your head is pounding with a hangover that is no longer cured by coffee and a big plate of bacon and eggs.'

Then I finished by thanking Rex for being the best life partner anyone could wish for and toasted our plans for the future. Even as I spoke those words, I knew they rang more with hope than with certainty. Perhaps, I thought by saying them out loud, in front of all these witnesses, it might stir in Rex the old enthusiasm he used to have for us and our life together.

The bowling club had a strict curfew of midnight, and at 11.30 every chair was empty—but to my absolute delight not one person had left, because Rory's list had worked its magic and the dancefloor was heaving. The old wooden floorboards threatened to collapse under the weight of all those feet stomping out the chorus in time with Nancy Sinatra's 'These Boots Are Made for Walking'.

Then I looked across to the bar and saw a solitary figure standing against it. Someone who hadn't danced once all night, who, when I'd tried to coax him up a couple of times, had fallen back on the old excuse of bad knees. After a few attempts I'd given up—I was having too much fun to care. Looking at him, it hit me. I felt loved by everyone in that room, with the possible exception of that one person at the bar.

Rex.

While the yawning staff were trying to pack us up and shut us down, two of my oldest friends from school, Justin and Artie, jumped up on a table and sang every verse of Barry McGuire's 60s protest song 'Eve of Destruction'. When it came to the chorus, we all drunkenly joined in.

My birthday party had buoyed me in a way I wasn't expecting. The reviews were unanimously positive, and for days afterwards I carried the triumph of the night with me. For most of our married life I had assumed that Rex was the drawcard in our partnership and that I was the addendum, that without him present no one would likely be interested in me. But as I flipped through the flashcard memories of that night, I saw a different picture. I had basked in the collective glow of my friends' admiration. I had stood alone in the limelight for the first time and found it to be a pretty life-affirming place. What's more, I had pulled off a fabulous party, with just one regret—I should have worn the Alannah Hill.

It was in the early aftermath of that success that I walked into Pillar of Salt Cafe near work to buy a take-away coffee. As I waited in the queue, I looked over at a woman who was eating breakfast alone and working on her computer. I found myself staring at her hair. I really liked it. The cut was not dissimilar to mine, except that it was a really pretty shade of rose blonde. I decided to go up to her and ask where she had it done. Turns out she was a hairdresser and did it herself, but she had her own set of life calamities going on and she wasn't taking new clients. We exchanged numbers anyway and I told her I'd wait. I said I'd been grey for ten years, so a few more months wouldn't matter.

A few days later, I got a text to say she might be able to squeeze me in on a cancellation if I was prepared to be flexible. Which I was.

So, on the 31st of May, after six hours in Samantha's chair, I come out all cropped and Katy Perry—and the very next week I am single and seriously questioning the adage that blondes have more fun.

Six hours in a home salon (that's how long it takes to go from grey to blonde) with someone you don't know might have been excruciating, especially since I am not great at small talk. But, despite the age difference of almost twenty years, Samantha and I established an instant and easy rapport. Turns out she doesn't do small talk either, so we cut straight to the grit of each other's life. Over the course of those hours I learnt that she was married to a guy she met in London during the party-fuelled 80s when she moved there to do hair and drugs. The relationship fell apart when they moved back to Australia and the party ended. Now, because the landlord wants to sell, she is being kicked out of the rented premises we're in today, which contains her home, her business and Sashie, her adorable big rescue dog. She has less than a month to find somewhere else to live and work. She asks me about my marriage and I find myself admitting to this virtual stranger something I've not given voice to before, that it's not going that well right now. I confess that I have not even told Rex that I am here being transformed and that I'm a little bit terrified of going home and fronting up as a blonde. I have a strong hunch that it won't be received all that favourably, nothing is these days. When I leave her, I am on a real high, not just because I like how I have turned out, but also because I feel I have met a promising new person, one who is curious and insightful, authentic and funny. As I'm about to turn into our street I see Rex and Heather walking towards the bowling club. I pull the car over and jump out to surprise him. He takes one look at me, shakes his head and walks on. Now when I replay that moment in my head, I imagine him sidling up to Anna at the club and saying, 'You won't believe what the stupid bitch has done now!'

Samantha calls me regularly to check on my hair and to make sure it hasn't taken a 'chickenish' (her term) yellow turn. She is more than a little surprised when on the third call, I tell her that my hair is fine, but I have been dumped by Rex and I'm currently staying with friends in Prahran. 'Oh Jo, I'm so sorry to hear that. I hope it wasn't the hair. That's right near L'Hotel Gitan,' she says. 'We could meet for a drink one night if you felt like it?'

I don't really feel like it, but I remember Terry's lesson and I force myself to make a date, just to get out. Besides it will be good to talk to someone who doesn't know me, or *us* and won't need a full post-mortem. I meet her at 6 pm on Tuesday of the following week, we order two glasses of pinot noir and sit at a bench with high stools. Again, the conversation flows really easily until she says, 'You know I fancy you.'

(Just so you know, my gaydar is terrible.)

'What do you mean? Are you gay? But you've just told me about your marriage breakup.'

'I'm bi.'

'Oh my god, but I'm the straightest person on the planet.'

'Not even curious?'

'No! I like men.'

'That's fine. We can still be friends, I just thought when you were staring at me in the cafe, you might have felt the same way.'

'No, no, no—I was staring at your hair!'

But despite my protestations, my mind and body launch me without warning into new and unchartered territory. My head is saying: well at least someone wants you, you're not completely washed up, and look at this woman, she is young and vibrant and voluptuous and her lips are pillowy soft and gorgeous. Which sets off a completely different response in my tingle territories. I feel an all-over charge course through my body and a pulsing between my legs that has produced moisture. I remember this sensation, it's called arousal, but what the hell am I supposed to do with it?

Go to the bathroom. That's what. So, I get up, make my way slowly and unsteadily through the tables of diners and drinkers, half hoping that Samantha will follow me in, push me up against the basin and pash me. Sadly, that doesn't happen, and when I get back to the table, I don't trust my feelings enough to say anything. So, we steer the conversation back to safer territory. But I drift home to Eve and Martin's that night acknowledging that I may have just had my first sexual stirrings since the breakup.

Good to know that I am not too old to get horny.

My sex life with Rex started well, better than well actually, matched as we were with an equal and frequent need for carnal expression. But as with most long-term relationships, it had lost the urgency that made it so compelling in the beginning. First it became more cuddlesome and couplish, we aroused and satisfied each other still, but it was more fireside than fireworks. Then, when Rex started taking antidepressants, he became a happier man to be with by day, but our night-life suffered the common side effect of libido loss. Rex hated it, but we found the price of an erection—meddling with the medication—a difficult balance to strike and ultimately not worth the cost. We accommodated for a time and later found a drug that supported intimacy but, by now, we were both more likely to lose ourselves, companionably side by side in the pages of a book than in the throes of passion. Later still in our relationship, when Rex was pulling away from me in other ways, intercourse became entwined with a fantasy that I found very distasteful. It entered our bedroom by stealth and was never spoken about in the light of day, but it sounded a death knell for our intimacy, and by silent consensus we virtually ceased to have sex at all. Or, should I say, Rex ceased to have sex with me. In a conversation we had soon after we separated, he asked me what I had been doing for sex all the while when we weren't having it: 'You must have had affairs surely?' 'No,' I told him, 'I had found ways to take care of myself.' He didn't want to believe that, mainly, I think, because he needed me to be complicit in his guilt.

So, for a very long time, my libido had been checked into a locker, languishing, and I wasn't even looking for the key. But the incident with Samantha reminded me that I was human and I was really missing human touch.

A cuddle, a back scratch, a foot rub. I remembered a masseur I'd visited several years ago who gave a particularly good version of 'one hour, full body' in a small studio above a cafe. I still had his number in my phone, so I gave him a call.

The next day, I walked up the set of stairs to the second floor and knocked on his door. The room was semi-dark, not the usual clinical white environment. No new-age music, no incense, no water fountains making you want to pee halfway through the massage. On the walls were objects from his personal life. Elsewhere in the room were a bicycle, a sideboard stacked with assorted plates and glasses, some clothes on hangers, a well-worn chesterfield couch and an old-fashioned stereo player with enormous speakers. In the middle: the massage table.

While we exchanged pleasantries, and I undressed behind a flimsy curtain, he told me that he was now married with two small boys. I told him I was now single, working through the fallout from that, and in need of a good massage. I saw a strange-looking booth at the end of the room that turned out to be a mini sauna and he invited me to go in and warm up. Unexpectedly he joined me in there. He was bare-chested and wearing tracksuit pants, I was wearing a towel. It was a little awkward, but to 'normalise' our semi-dressed proximity we continued to talk as if we were two friends sitting across from each other at a cafe. He told me he now split his time between his home on the coast and this room, where he stayed occasionally during the week.

After ten minutes or so, we got out and I lay face down on the table, naked. He put on some light classical music and started by dry brushing my back. Don't know if you have ever experienced that, but it's like a million ants in stilettos crawling all over your skin—delicate but deeply satisfying and wildly moreish. You will them to go everywhere. You want them to multiply and stampede. You don't ever want them to stop.

When they unfortunately did, a soft blanket was thrown over me and slowly, slowly pulled off down the length of my body. In my mind, I was having a conversation with myself. Where is this going? Is it okay? Am I safe here? Should I be on high alert? Should I do what my brain is telling me to do, or should I let my body win this time?

Then he touches me and there's no going back. Warm fragrant oil, sure expert pressure, atmospheric piano music in a darkened room. I'm no longer in Melbourne, I'm in a European film, in an attic. There could be a war raging outside. Indeed, I have been through my own version of war. But in here, I am safe. I am in good hands. I am other.

The touch is therapeutic. It is remedial. It is replenishing. At some point, I let it cross over into sensual. I do this consciously, reframing my masseur as an anonymous lover rather than a paid therapist. The voice in my head says, 'Go with it, Jo.' What's the worst that can happen? I am relaxed and I am oily and I am giving myself over to the pleasure of this moment—because it is so unlike anything that has ever happened to me before, and I want new things to happen. I want this to happen.

When I turn over onto my back, I am sure my desire must be as naked as I am.

The professional hands keep finding knots, working slowly, methodically. Head, neck, shoulders, arms, left, right, chest, breasts, abdomen. Long rhythmic strokes. This is beyond massage, it is exquisite foreplay and he knows it. When he gets to my upper thigh it is too much, my back arches.

'Feel what you have done to me,' I say.

That's where he draws the line. 'Sorry, I can't do that.'

But I can't not do it. My climax has become a physical imperative. While he continues massaging my feet, there is tacit agreement that I can. I don't think I have ever felt more heightened, more liquid. I touch myself and set off an almighty release that doesn't stop with my sex organs. It shatters my whole body. While I shudder and sob, he noiselessly continues to massage and soothe.

At last he says, 'I think you needed that.'

In the car driving home I am suffused with heat, nerve endings arcing wildly and absurdly unembarrassed. I had just masturbated in front of a stranger. And instead of feeling shame I felt like a cigarette and a gin and tonic.

Who is this person?

Where did she come from?

At home with the gin and tonic in hand, but foregoing the cigarette, I wonder how he is feeling after that? Did I leave him with a hard-on? Did he have to masturbate the minute I left, or is this simply his thing? A niche market he has found in his professional offering. A forte that sits within the bounds of the law, but outside the realms of the norm. Facilitating but not 'participating in' sex.

A month later I swallow my pride and book another appointment. I have to find out.

Back in that room, my secret refuge, so remote from the real world, it seamlessly happens again. The touch relaxes, the mind lets go of objection, the music transports. There is implicit permission and complete absence of judgment. This swarthy semi-handsome man of uncertain age and unknown ethnicity is a master of anatomy, a maestro of touch, and through him I've found the sex I can have without having sex.

PART 2
Recalibration

While I am trying to navigate this new reality, so too is Rex. Evidently, he is having as much trouble as I am coping without the certainties of life that kept us entwined and gave us purpose. The nightly dinner call, the shared household chores, Saturday morning bike rides, caring for Heather, coffee at Magic Cafe, epic battles on the golf course. These things, while each unremarkable on its own, added up to something reliable and reassuring we could fall back on. While they didn't compensate for the confusion of our end-of-relationship emotions, they did represent the stable order of our ongoing affection. Now we are both having to relearn how to 'do life' without the security of the other one being in it. On one hand, Rex's guilt is alleviated by his admission, but on the other, he's left himself with a not-too-well-planned new life to navigate. And me the same.

While Charles and Diana had the off-camera Camilla as the destructive third partner in their marriage, we had Rex's depression. It was there long before Anna came along, visiting us with erratic regularity and unpredictable severity, playing havoc with our plans and our daily lives, threatening the veneer of our domestic harmony. It resurfaces for Rex now and takes a devastating stranglehold.

I know this because he calls to tell me he has been classified a suicide risk and put on watch. I am supposed to be shocked. I am supposed to rush to his aid. At the very least, I am expected to try couples' therapy, which is what he says he now wants.

Again, I am torn, my devotion tested, but I am reminded of how often Rex's depression and the fallout from it has been my mess to clean up. I have lived with being locked out by this beast, whose name cannot be mentioned, whose existence is denied, whose pathology lies in wait to strike with maximum damage, who calls the shots. But for once I don't prioritise the demands of Rex and his demon illness over my own wellbeing. I will not drop everything and rush to his aid when for so long he chose to ignore the signs that were so plain to see and so doggedly refused my help or to help himself.

Instead, knowing he is in safe hands with his doctor, I suggest we could meet for a drink when he feels better.

It's 5.30, mid-winter, already dark, and as I enter the bar I see him sitting there, dwarfed inside his big navy woollen overcoat, head bent checking his phone. My infuriating, funny, deceitful, addictive friend of thirty years.

He looks ravaged and small, clearly diminished by the strain. As I approach, my impulse is to hug him, to hold him tight, tell him everything will be all right. But I remind myself that we are here, on this fresh battlefield, in this new war, because of choices he made. So, as I sit down, we keep to our newly established social distance and try to ignore the fact that we know each other's deepest fears and darkest secrets intimately.

He must be fighting the same irresistible pull of familiarity, because he says, 'Just say the word, Jo, and I will take us home, pick up our passports, drive to the airport and go anywhere you want.'

This is torture for me because in these early days—when our breakup is fresh, when I still feel like Rex's wife, when not enough time has elapsed for me to be anything else—that's exactly what I want. To be *us* again. To be going somewhere together. Taking off on one of our planned big adventures. Taking risks with the assurance that together we'll be okay.

But then my thoughts go to the other person he is also making promises to. I know that if I agree to do what he wants—what I want—the minute we board the plane, he will be thinking of her. As we buckle our seatbelts, I will see the shadow cross his face. Wherever he is, I imagine he wants to be in the elsewhere. The closer he gets to someone, the stronger is his attraction to the one slipping away.

It's not the first time it's happened in our relationship, but it's the first time I haven't fought to save us. I wrestle with a titanic internal struggle, but I finally manage to kill my desire and tell him 'no'.

As we walk away in opposite directions that night, we both carry a sadness that feels so heavy we can barely lift our feet. Me because I have been offered a get-out-of-jail-free card and I didn't take it. Rex because he has played his trump card and it didn't take the trick.

The next day Martin finds an envelope with my name on it that has been pushed under the door. I recognise Rex's handwriting instantly. I take it upstairs to read in the privacy of my room. Inside is a single typed sheet of paper:

>**Sorry**
>
>I am sorry for not respecting you more.
>I am sorry for not respecting myself more.
>I am sorry for taking our life together for granted.
>I am sorry for closing myself off emotionally.
>I am sorry for betraying your trust.
>I am sorry for jeopardising our future life together.
>I am sorry for not sharing more of myself with you.
>I am sorry for not being more receptive to future travel plans and shared experiences.

> I am sorry for not trying to save our marriage.
> I am sorry for becoming physically and emotionally involved with another person.
> I am sorry for the pain and distress I have caused you.
> I am sorry for the hurt and anxiety I have caused our family and friends.
> I am sorry for being so selfish.
> I am sorry that I showed so little regard for our history together.
> I am sorry I stopped talking to you.
> I am sorry I let go of the embrace of our minds.
> I am sorry I didn't confide in you that I needed help.
> I am sorry I fucked up our lives.

My heart lurches with every line. I take this letter to Terry, secretly hoping that she will say he deserves another chance. Instead, she says, 'Jo, these are words. What are his actions telling you? Has he stopped seeing the other girl? He hasn't said so. Has he told her it is over and that he is committed to repairing his marriage? Has he tried to help himself to understand the "why" behind his sorry life? Until he *shows* you sorry, you can be pretty damned sure he's not sorry enough.'

Normally I leave my sessions with Terry feeling not better necessarily but bolstered in a way that enables me to go on. Today I feel defeated, devoid of fight, wishing for obliteration. Driving back to Eve and Martin's, I wonder, is Terry always right? Why do I so fervently want her to be wrong on this one? Those words, admittedly only words, are a salve to my deceived and humiliated self and a boost to my badly bruised ego. In that list, Rex has said everything I wanted to hear. He has owned his guilt, admitted his failings, pushed all my hot buttons (*embrace of our minds*) and flushed my stubbornly blocked forgiveness vein. But, it's true, he has not told me the one thing I need to know if we are to have any chance of repairing our marriage. It's not something I can ask him either, because how can I trust him not to lie, or not even lie necessarily, but act on an impulse that is fleeting and unreliable? Rex is very skilled at knowing what I need to hear and at controlling the narrative to suit himself. In this vulnerable state, where I risk casting a wrong vote, I choose instead to abstain. If Rex is committed to getting back together, surely I should test his resolve by waiting a few weeks. And I should wait to see if it matters enough to him, if *I* matter enough to him, for him to end it with Anna.

In the meantime, I spend my abundant spare time cataloguing all the things I miss about him. One of the first I discover is that after you have lived with someone for thirty years, you don't just miss the person, you miss the presence. I feel the empty air beside me when I walk; I hear the silence beside me in the car; in bed there is nothing between me and the wall. There is a void in my life that can't be touched, but I can feel its outlines.

Then I go to the small intimacies we aggregated over the course of our married life, the banter and repartee we trademarked as ours. What to do with those now that their use-by date has seemingly come and gone. Our favourite journalistic clichés: 'What's happened to Sam Stosur? Bundled out in the first round.' 'How big were the hailstones? As big as golf balls.' Or the comment Rex never failed to make every time I'd overreach on the golf course and attempt a shot beyond my skill: 'Million-dollar swing, ten-cent brain.' I'd no longer nestle in under his arm for a 'wingy'. I'd no longer be the Smurf to his Felix.

Referring to my nickname, I once said to Rex, 'You have very high expectations of something made of blue plastic.' I wonder if he's lowered his expectations for *her*.

It's true, the sudden absence of the person and the familiar patterns takes as much getting used to as the emotional devastation that has been wrought through the sudden separation of long conjoined minds. So perhaps it's no surprise that one day when I am rushing to get to work and I fall down a step at Eve and Martin's place, fracturing my ankle, I instinctively pick up my phone to call the person I love. Then I remember, that person loves someone else, and I put the phone down.

While I lie on the couch at Eve and Martin's with my moon-booted leg elevated on a cushion, feeling more sorry for myself than usual, I address the need to balance the ledger. I take out my notebook to list all the things I don't miss about Rex. Top of the list: those intimidating moods and impenetrable silences that might last for days. Like the time we were underbidders for a house Rex really wanted to buy in Nott Street, Port Melbourne. I liked it too, but didn't form quite the same emotional attachment that Rex did. He had decided it was 'the one'. Come auction day, it seemed that half of Melbourne had decided the same thing. The bidding spiralled upwards at a perilous pace and we quickly reached our limit. After a hastily convened huddle, we decided to go higher, made the bid, and watched as the hammer came down once, and then once more—we were about to buy our (well, Rex's) dream home—when just before the third and final knockdown of the hammer, a knockout bid came from nowhere. In the space of two seconds, we went from triumphant new homeowners to wound-licking underbidders.

I was disappointed of course, but my much greater concern was how I would manage Rex's disappointment. It was immense and palpable. It's not overstatement to say that as we drove home in a thick silence, I was scared of the lit fuse burning towards his anger tank. Would he take it out on me, himself, the apartment he no longer wanted to live in. I feared a physical reaction, instead I got menacing silence. Our pre-emptive celebratory champagne warmed. Night fell. Dinner remained unprepared. Any consolatory utterance was immediately incinerated by the intensity of his heat. Eventually I went to bed, thinking and hoping it might be better the next day. It wasn't. The silence lasted for three days and only when my fear morphed into frustration, did Rex come around. Until then, I had placated, tolerated, even empathised with 'his' loss.

But, seriously, why was this necessary? I know I signed up for a lot when I married Rex, but the job description for wife was constantly being edited, and mood manager was rapidly becoming one of my primary roles. For a task I didn't enjoy, it was taking up way too much of my time and energy. I'd look around me at other relationships and, although you can never really know what goes on inside the confines of other couples' walls, I felt certain the couples I knew weren't performing these sorts of gymnastics just to maintain an accord.

Next, I listed his volatility. Those public displays of anger that often left me speechless and mortified. Once we were in a glasses shop where I had shortlisted three sets of frames. I called him over to ask his opinion and was disappointed when he chose the most conservative. Secretly I was hoping he'd corroborate my choice, the square blue frames with the tortoiseshell finish, the ones the assistant and I had already placed at number one. When I said as much to Rex, he made a loud scene in the shop, shouting at me to buy whatever fucking frames I liked and if I didn't want his opinion why did I ask in the first place? Then he stormed out, leaving the assistant and me with nowhere to look but at each other and everyone else in the shop looking at us.

Eventually she said, 'Well, I still like them,' and I said, 'So do I.' Then we cracked up laughing in that conspiratorial way women do when grown men lose control of their inner child. It was my act of defiance that day to stay behind and order them: usually, I would dismiss my own feelings, pursue him, and try to smooth the waters. In an even more bizarre postscript: about eighteen months after we separated, Rex and I had to co-sign some legal papers, and for the sake of expedience, I agreed to meet him at our old place as long as I didn't have to go inside. Rex brought the papers out to my car and I couldn't help noticing he was wearing new glasses. He'd chosen those exact same frames!

That volatility underpinned our daily lives. Passive/aggressive is only the beginning of a long list of emotional dissonances I learned to live with: generous/withholding; loquacious/mute; I'm here for you/I'm not interested; I care about you/I couldn't care less; we're a team/stop suffocating me; help me/leave me alone. With Rex you learned to take the good with the bad and you were never really sure what you'd get. I was the fulcrum on which these moods turned. I was the junkie and he was the unreliable supplier of my hits. I suffered the withdrawals because I was addicted to the highs. While our bad times were bleak and solitary, our good times were shared with an exuberance that was equal and elevating. We loved taking long road trips, anywhere really, but especially to Port Fairy where our competitiveness came along for the ride and rendered everything a good-natured contest. Who had the best stamina behind the wheel, who put together the best playlist, who'd take home the green jacket after a three-day tournament on the golf course. Where would we go for dinner with so many great choices in town. Fine dining at Fen, pizza at Coffin Sally, the Merrijig Kitchen, the Victoria Hotel. We loved them all and agreed, the daily winner got to choose.

As I continue to nurse my injured ankle, I have plenty of time to reflect on the pros and cons of Rex, but I also have a pressing need to get mobile again.

For two hours, twice a week, yoga had been my drug of choice. It took me out of my head and provided the mental space and physical exertion I needed to help me sleep. When our teacher Sabine announces she's taking a group to Bali in August, I eagerly sign up—partly because I know the yoga will be good for me, but mainly because I love to travel, and without my travel companion of the last thirty years, I'm not sure I could go it alone. Sabine has presented a convenient opportunity to get back to a place I love, to do something I enjoy, and be with a ready-made group of buddies, including best mates Eve and Martin.

That's when, two weeks out from the trip, I misjudge their bottom step, ending up in the Emergency Department at Cabrini. Fortunately, it's a small spiral fracture in my left leg where I already have some pretty heavy-duty hardware from a previous cycling accident in Spain. I tell the surgeon of my travel plans—playing down the yoga part—and he gives me the all-clear to go as long as I'm careful and agree to wear my knee-high moon boot at all times, except in bed.

It's not ideal, but it's not all bad either. The first bonus comes at the airport gate when I am upgraded to business class for more leg room. And the next day, when we hit the mats, I discover that there are some advantages to doing yoga in a boot, although not many. You are excused from trikonasana (my least favourite pose), you get to do legs up the wall (a lot) and, miraculously, you can do inversions (my favourites) because they're not weight-bearing. Well, not leg weight-bearing, anyway.

But the real bonus comes in the stories that we share over communal meals. Banish any preconception you might have of a yoga retreat being all austere, inward-gazing and alcohol-free. This is far from the case with Sabine's retreats, and we quickly establish that once the work is done, the fun can come. In our private open-air restaurant, set among the rice paddies, we're free to eat, talk and share life stories. Francesca is further into her marriage split than me and assures me that once I can embrace the freedom of making my own decisions and inhabiting my own space, I'll love it and probably never want to give it up. Greta, a practising Buddhist and family counsellor, gives me some sound advice about using the situation for some self-investigation and offers some helpful reading recommendations (Pema Chödrön and Esther Perel), while Peggy, an older woman whose husband left her years ago, pulls me aside and says, 'Take a lover, Jo—or several—it will do wonders for your confidence.'

This is my first experience of the sisterhood in action, and all of a sudden I understand its power.

I'd made a deal with myself, and with Eve and Martin, that when I came back from Bali, I'd start to look for a place of my own.

For two months, I'd been cocooned in the safe haven of their home and it was time to cut the cord. I started to look at apartments online, but it had been about thirty-five years since I'd rented and things had certainly changed. For starters, you don't go to the agent and pick up a key anymore: you line up with thirty other hopefuls, and if you want to apply, you need to complete this exhaustive online form which completely does my head in. Then it quickly becomes apparent that the size of the line is directly proportional to the desirability of the property. One morning, I arrived early at an inspection in Richmond all cock-a-hoop because I was the only person there, but soon discovered that was because the place stank of cat's piss and had mould from ceiling to floor. And it was $450 a week. Clearly, I'd need to change my criteria—and my budget.

It was at this desultory point in my search that Rex phoned and sheepishly informed me that Anna would be moving in. I was literally sitting in my car outside that shitty rental when the call came through. Here was I contemplating life with a mouldy bathroom, while Anna would soon be showering under my rainhead fitting, and drying herself with a warm towel from the heated towel racks we installed last year.

He goes on to explain that he knows this is not ideal because all my stuff is still there and we haven't even begun the painful process of divvying up. But 'poor Anna' has nowhere to go. Her husband has gone back to England and she can't afford to stay in her apartment on her own.

I suggest he could move in with her, and without a trace of irony, he says, 'I couldn't live there; it's a dog box.'

I've no inclination to make this easy for them, but if I am ever to move on with my life, this next hurdle has to be faced. So, even though we have not yet touched on the formal separation of assets, I agree to meet Rex at our home in Dorcas Street one Sunday afternoon to attempt a civil separation of our domestic possessions. Fortunately, Heather is not here to compound the grief. I'd already said my goodbyes to her a few weeks earlier when Rex phoned to say he was taking her back to Guide Dogs Victoria slightly ahead of schedule, because he'd felt unable to care for her properly in his reduced state.

Now he needs me and my stuff out, so 'poor Anna'

will have a proper home to live in. To even attempt to get through the day, I have to minimise that thought—hit the yellow button as I would on my Mac, and park it in a far corner of my mind—because the absurd thing is, here I am standing in my kitchen, where I cooked so many delicious meals for us and fabulous dinners for our neighbours and friends, but today I'm not menu-planning, I'm looking at my blender and my fruit bowl (now containing two shrivelled lemons) and my sideboard stacked with recipe books and wondering if he will let me take these things? Rex is sitting in his usual position on the other side of the bench and we are both uncertain how to start. While I've stalled at an emotional impasse, he seems to be more business driven, not wanting to press, but eager to get things done. So I hand him the list I've prepared of the things I really want—some mainly for sentimental reasons—and Rex doesn't argue. Hard to really, when his new girlfriend's belongings are piled up behind the closed door of 'our' spare bedroom. I don't go in there, not this time, anyway.

As I pull out drawers and open cupboards Rex is vigilantly there, making sure I don't take anything that's not mine, like Nanna Salmon's Spode bowl, a gift carried over from his first wedding, or more than my fair share. Sets of eight plates are pointlessly divided in half so that I get four and he gets four—no matter, I'll probably never host a dinner party for eight again. The fact that they are mostly pieces I have collected over the years is not taken into consideration. As the day drags on, I find myself caring less about things, which can easily be replaced, and wondering more about what we have lost and why. But Rex is in no mood for sentimentality, so eventually we get through all the banalities like crockery and cookware, Christmas decorations, camping gear, linen, furnishings and tools without incident, and I pile up my half in the dining room to be collected once I have found my own place. Well, almost without incident. For my fiftieth birthday, Eliza gave me a set of six lead cut-crystal champagne flutes from the Museum of Modern Art in New York. Nothing like Nanna's lead cut crystal, they were works of art themselves and I loved them, but as I don't believe in using things only for 'good', there were only two left intact, and while we were packing and stacking, Rex broke one. That left me with just one, the significance of which was not lost on me.

The last task for the day is the splitting of our shared photo albums and our co-written travel journals. Our life together in words and pictures. Here, I expect an argument. There are lots to get through, so I suggest we take turns to choose from the shelves. But in the most painful episode of a day that's already had so many, he cursorily flicks through the albums, removes about five pictures in total and tells me I can keep the rest. The past, evidently, holds no interest for him.

I am still in my moon boot and my ankle is throbbing like a madman. The day has taken an enormous toll, mentally and physically.

As I drive back to Eve and Martin's place, I sink to my lowest point yet. How can so much time together be dismissed so summarily?

Five fucking pictures!

I sit and think about what's just transpired. While we'd been upstairs in the office with the albums and journals, I had, rather pathetically, turned to Rex and asked him not to forget me. He'd given a pat answer: 'Of course I won't.' But in that moment, I'd really needed more. I'd needed him to say that this was hard for him too, that our life together had meant something, that the memories contained in this room would stay with him forever. Because there's a difference between not wanting to go back to him and not wanting to be 'wiped'. But that's what was happening: I was simply being wiped from his life. Cancelled. Maybe it was his pride protecting him, keeping my feelings out, keeping his in.

I had felt acutely that this day, alone together for the final time in our final home, was our chance to call a cease-fire, set hostilities aside and acknowledge the loss on both sides. But Rex had remained remote all day, steely, eerily unemotional, just wanting to get it done and get me out of there. A far cry from the proposal made in the bar less than two months ago. Seems Terry was right after all: actions speak louder than words. I'd received no further 'proof' from Rex that he cared enough to make *us* work. In fact, in the space of that short time, I had been consigned to history. Anna had been officially instated as 'the new (child) bride', leaving me, with the emotions and memories dredged up by this day, feeling annihilated all over again.

Back at Eve and Martin's, grief hits me like a speeding car that missed the stop sign. I'm T-boned by loss and loneliness and the now absolute finality of it. Alone in my upstairs room, I unravel unreservedly, tears threatening to burst the reservoir. I didn't know it at the time, and perhaps Rex's cool indifference helped, but on this day the high watermark was reached, and slowly, drop by drop, the water and the grief start to subside.

Terry advises me to do nothing in haste and to avoid making any big decisions for the first twelve months. This seems sensible to me, as my mind's changing every two minutes and my mood swings are parabolic, but I no longer have the fallback of waiting for an outcome. Rex and I are history.

I restart my rental search in earnest, grateful that on top of the many challenges I face going into this new life phase, financial stress is not one of them. Within reason I have the luxury to find a 'nice place', which I finally do, and even though I submit an early application, and on paper I think I am the ideal tenant, I lose out to 'a young couple'. Yes, take a knife and stab me in the heart, real estate agent Jennifer.

I am supposed to be comforted by the fact that I came

second, but I am more discomforted by the fact that the world sees me differently. As a single older woman, I am somehow diminished. Where is my husband? What calamity has brought me back to renting after all this time? Might I be unpredictable, unstable? Suddenly, I am not a safe pick—I'm an outlier.

However, a few days later, I receive a call from Jennifer, letting me know that the owners have changed their mind because, it transpires, 'the perfect young couple' have a not-so-perfect dog. One prejudice trumps another it seems. So, if I am still interested, the place is mine. A quick flash of pride tempts me to tell them to stick their pokey little apartment up their arse, but the search has been long, I am weary, and I am in need of some independence. Besides, in my mind, I have already furnished and decorated the place, which is like a cosy little ski chalet, except that it's in suburban South Yarra. I say yes.

September 15. Almost three months to the day since life as I knew it ended—and life as I have never experienced it is about to begin.

I have never lived alone and, since the age of eighteen, I have very rarely even been single, so I am terrified and excited in equal measure. I am about to discover what it's like not to be 'Rex and Jo', not even 'Eve and Martin and Jo', but just Jo.

Who even is that?

This is my chance to do the work I baulked at when I

was forty, last time I was separated from Rex. I know the extra twenty years have changed me in so many ways—age does that. For starters I'm certainly a more confident person than I used to be, thanks to Eliza's positive influence and the fact of us having run our own business for most of that time. And probably, with more sunsets under my belt, I'm better equipped to confront my failings. But, it's one thing to arrive voluntarily at the decision to 'find yourself' and quite another having the necessity of it thrust upon you by adverse circumstances.

Before I can do anything though, I have to move in. And to move in, I have to collect all my stuff from Dorcas Street, where Rex now lives with Anna. No way I can do this alone, so I enlist the help of two good mates. Genevieve is the friend I discovered the world with, way back in 1980. We met at university and bonded for life when we were both dumped, unceremoniously and simultaneously, by our then boyfriends and I ended up sleeping on a mattress on Gen's bedroom floor in Clifton Hill. We were matching basket cases, feeling the youthful sting of rejection and the certainty that no one would ever love us again. So bad was our despair that we were prescribed Mogadon in order to get through the night and subsequently to front up for work the next day, Gen teaching English at Gladstone Park High and me making sandwiches and spanakopita at John's Gourmet Food in Domain Road. Lord knows what genius doctor prescribed addictive sedatives to twenty-four year-old girls, but with the support and friendship we found in each other, we were able to kick the pills, relegate those loser boyfriends to history and go in search of the next big adventure. Which happened to be an overland trip from Indonesia to Europe, where our eyes were progressively opened wider and wider by, among other things, magic mushrooms sold in little baskets and cooked any way you like in any cafe in Jogjakarta, pie shops selling amazing lemon meringue pies and high-grade hashish in Kathmandu, elegant coffee shops serving wine and pastries all day in Paris, and the inconvenience of the siesta in Spain which made dinnertime way too late for us (only a problem insofar as our financial circumstances and our desire to remain skinny only permitted two meals a day). And then, of course, there was the scary stuff like tour guides toting machine guns in Burma, and the mind-boggling array of penises on display at Super Paradise beach in Mykonos. Genevieve is the sister I never had and a natural ally to have by my side today.

Francie came to me via Rex (she's one of the best things he gave me) and has rapidly ascended the ranks to be one of my all-time favourite people. Apart from being my partner in the game of 'Which would you choose?' (Sex with John Howard or Tony Abbot? Wake up blind or deaf? Eat snot or garden snails?) and many meaning-of-life discussions on long bike rides, she is the very essence of industry and practicality. Today, she brings the textas, the tape gun, the cleaning agents, the newspaper, the labels and the wicked humour that will make light work of the day's tasks. We meet the removal van at 9.30 in the morning—when Rex and Anna are both safely elsewhere.

Before we start, though, we check out the changes that have taken place. Curiously, there is now a colour photograph of cows in a paddock above my bed, where a black and white still from the film *The Piano* used to hang. Plus, we can't help noticing the scrunched-up tissues and thick layer of dust on the bedhead. In my cupboards, there is an unfamiliar collection of clothes, lots of lumberjack check, a Hollie Hobbie doll and some books on veganism (I pray she's a vegan so Rex will have to curb his bi-weekly lamb chop habit). There are long black hairs in the bathroom basin, some original 'artworks' under the stairs, and, leaning against the wall in the shed where my well-travelled Pinarello used to be, there's a pink bike with a plastic basket, a bell and multi-coloured streamers.

Most of her stuff is still crammed into the second bedroom and we feel justified opening the door just a crack, to further assess her taste in clothes and furniture. Genevieve suggests nipping over to South Melbourne market and buying a bag of prawns to bury deep at the back of the wardrobe. The suggestion titillates us all, but the thought of it is enough. I have Michele Obama in my ear saying, 'Never allow yourself to stoop to their level.'

While we pack and carry and label and laugh, a day that

should have been unbearable is actually quite good fun. It is a comfort to me that Rex will not be surrounded by the good taste he once enjoyed, as most of it is moving with me to South Yarra. I deliberately crossed over the Great Divide of St Kilda Road to ensure I wouldn't be regularly running into him and Anna. And most of what he has gained seems to be straight from a student house—good to know youth has some drawbacks.

I've had to trade South Melbourne market for Prahran, and the Bay for the Botanic Gardens, but I've signed a twelve-month lease on a very cute 80s apartment with exposed internal beams and a suspended spiral staircase that wobbles when you climb it. It leads to my favourite room, the big mezzanine bedroom, full of space, light and the welcoming waft of freshly laid carpet. Upstairs, to my great relief, there's also a newly renovated, mould-free bathroom and a second bedroom that will be home to guests, junk and yoga gear. Through floor-to-ceiling glass doors downstairs, I look out on a generous private courtyard with a disconcerting wall of mirror at one end; it amplifies the size of the space, but gives me a fright every time I catch sight of someone in it, someone who, curiously, so far has always turned out to be me. There's a brick wall covered in thick green ficus and some small garden beds where I'll be able to cultivate herbs and rocket. Importantly, it's close to Eve and Martin, close to work, and close to Ned's Bake. I can walk everywhere and compensate myself with Ned's amazing almond croissants. As far as places to road-test singledom go, this seems to be ticking a lot of boxes.

By day's end, my little urban ski lodge is well on the way to being set up. Francie, who took charge of the kitchen, has cleaned shelves, lined drawers, found the right place for everything and arranged my knick-knacks almost exactly as I would have myself. She has squashed boxes, filled bins and loaded her own car with rubbish to take it away so I don't have to deal with it. We are filthy and completely trashed. What these women have done for me today goes beyond any gratitude I can express. They have not just helped me move from one house to another, but from one life to another.

I have done the countback and, since uni days, I have lived in sixteen different houses and eleven suburbs. But this was the one move I didn't see coming.

Genevieve brings an inflatable mattress and a sleeping bag and stays the night in the spare room so I am not alone. We have a simple meal and way too many wines at Ned's and reminisce—as we always do when we are together—about 1980, our amazing year of discovery and enlightenment. I'm sure it gets better with every retelling—we become more intrepid, our adventures more daring, our highlight reel more spectacular—but tonight, for the first time, it feels possible that events that are this life-defining may not be confined exclusively to the past. Just maybe, if I can dig up that person I was back then, there may be more to come.

All the big-ticket items are left at Dorcas Street to be tallied as part of the formal separation. Vestiges of my former life which I have no wish to be reminded of by allowing them to take up residence in my new place. Instead, I have the bittersweet joy of working with a blank canvas, so I sit down in my one borrowed chair and draw up a shopping list that is a retailer's dream. Top of the list, of course, is a new smart TV—followed by a sofa, dining table and chairs, bed and bedding, fridge, washing machine, microwave, barbeque, vacuum cleaner, kitchenware—and an industrial-strength corkscrew, for all the sorrows I intend to be drowning. The hit to my credit card is hefty and made all the more galling by the fact that, of course, I already own all these things. But I consider it an investment in my future, one that will pay dividends I hope, in the uncertain months and years ahead.

As I face the wall of TVs all showing Kochie's sweaty head in frightening clarity, I think, *How do I choose a TV on my own?* Electronics was always Rex's department. But when the sales assistant approaches and asks what size I'm thinking of, I experience the small thrill of not having to compromise. Rex was no different from most men in that when it came to TVs, size definitely mattered. Regardless of room size, proportion or aesthetics, it seemed you just had to get as up-close and personal with Buddy or Danger or Roughie or Pendles as possible. And, bottom line, it just had to be bigger than the bloke-next-door's.

So I reply, 'Show me the smallest, smartest, most beautiful TV you have.'

As the deliveries begin to arrive and these carefully chosen items start to populate and personalise my space, they provide some consolation, but they are no match for my newest unwelcome companion: aloneness. It asserts itself in my life as a constant presence where companionship and contentment used to hang out. And it brings along a nasty little sidekick called silence. These two gang up on me and taunt me while I sit, alone, on my new orange two-seater sofa, staring in silence at my lifeless smart TV, yet to be turned on and tuned in. *Loser. Who's gonna love you now, loser? Cooking for one tonight, loser? What are you doing on the weekend, loser?*

Singularity is not my natural state.

Here's a confronting prospect. It's late November, work has been really busy, and end-of-year party invitations are coming in thick and fast. But after the flurry of activity is over and everyone disbands to do their own thing, I have no plans. I've never been a big fan of Christmas, all that forced bonhomie, unwrapping of things you don't like or need, calling forth academy-award acting performances to convey the exact opposite, preceded by the compulsion to buy gifts for others that they most likely won't need or like either. Eliza calls me the Christmas Grinch, which is fair enough, but even so, I don't relish the idea of spending two long weeks alone in an empty city with no one to even pull a cracker with.

My family is small and scattered. I have two brothers, but only one that I see. The other one lives a self-imposed reclusive existence in northern New South Wales. My mother and father are both long dead and, to be honest, Rex and I always spent much more time with his family, who were Christmas crazy, than we did with mine at this time of year. But Roy, my closer brother (still eleven years my senior), and his wife, Janine, who I haven't seen in ages, are having Christmas with their kids and grandkids in Margaret River where they now live, and they invite me to come along. Our bond is strong, having been forged when, as a newly married couple, they lived with Dad and me, right after Mum died. Janine was twenty-one, Roy was twenty-two, and I was the kid that was foist upon them when they were really just kids themselves. At the time, their presence in the house distracted me from my sadness and made life bearable.

No, that's unfair: it was better than bearable. It was really quite good fun to have such young people as my quasi-parents. We'd go to the local footy every Saturday and while Roy played, Janine and I served pies, chips and hot coffee from the local canteen. If we heard the car horns honking, we'd look up to see who'd scored the goal and who was in front. Post-match post-mortems with pea soup and friends were a weekly highlight and I felt privileged to be included in their adult world. I went everywhere with them: camping, the Croydon drive-in (*Doctor Zhivago* was a special highlight), Tupperware parties, car rallies. I was the serial pest that never left their side and their nickname for me was Harper. Harper Jo, because I was always wanting more of those good times and I'd harp hard if I wasn't included.

No wonder they went west.

Roy was a carpenter by trade and there was big money to be made building in Western Australia in the 70s. So, after three years living with Dad and me, they bought a brand-new ice-blue Ford Falcon, which I thought was the coolest car I'd ever seen, drove out of our driveway for the last time and headed across the Nullarbor to make their fame and fortune, while I waved and cried and clung to my dad. The first Christmas they were away, I was allowed to go visit them in Exmouth. I was thirteen and I flew by myself to Perth, where I stayed overnight with friends of theirs (people I didn't know) who, next morning, put me on a Pioneer Coach headed up the Brand Highway.

I felt so grown-up, so brave to be travelling this huge distance alone, so excited to see them and, I remember, so mesmerised by the barren desert landscape out the bus window that barely changed for eight hours.

Now here I am, forty-eight years later, alone again, booking a Christmas Eve flight to Perth, to spend Christmas with Janine and Roy and plonk myself in the middle of a happy hectic scene that, it turns out, reveals my extended family to me in a whole new light.

On the four-hour bus ride from Perth airport to Margaret River, I have plenty of time to get anxious. The thread of familiarity has been broken by distance and time, so we will need to get to know each other all over again. And I am still grappling with my new single status. One good thing about Rex was his gift for sociability. He could enter a room and immediately break down the barriers of reticence, establishing an easy and natural rapport with people from all walks of life, strangers and kids included. He'd remember things about them too, specifics that would provide a ready conversation starter and flatter them with his interest. He'd talk barramundi fishing with my nephew Troy and ask my niece Lucinda about her foot (injured years earlier in a tractor accident). I'm sure my family looked forward to seeing Rex more than they did me, only this time we'd have to blunder through without him. Roy meets me at the bus stop and with one big bear hug, those fears are laid to rest. As we pull apart, we both have tears in our eyes and even though we will still have to find new bridges, I know everything will be all right. History and blood will see to that.

There's a joke in the west that WA stands for 'windy always' or 'wait awhile'. Both are true. Nothing happens fast, and along with the blinding glare of the unfiltered sun there is always a freshening wind in the afternoon which has given rise to Roy's rule—never leave home after 4 pm without a jumper. So, in the dazzling, leisurely days and cool evenings that follow I learn to SUP (Stand Up Paddle) on the Margaret River, I swim in the Indian Ocean, and discover that it is truly the colour of Indian ink. I run along the rugged coastal cliffs with Lucinda, struggling to keep up and catch up on her life at the same time. I get to know her daughters, who I register are my great nieces, babies last time I saw them, now of an age where their divergent emerging personalities are fascinating. I spend a night at Troy's place in Dawesville where he takes me out in his pride and joy, 'The Bar Crusher', to check the craypots. We pull in three beauties and one empty shell that has already made a feast for an opportunistic octopus. I meet his new partner, Billie, who flies back from her shift in Tom Price early to spend time with the mysterious Aunty Jo from the east. Troy cooks fish he has caught himself and picks a bag of home-grown chillies for me take home. In between the fun and the laughter, I reminisce with Roy and Janine about those early days after Mum died, thanking them for including me in their lives and apologising for being such a pain. Disappointingly, they don't contradict me on that.

How did I let these people go? Why don't I know them better? I have precious little in the way of family, so why haven't I kept them closer?

Could be that after they left to go west the first time, I became too accustomed to being on my own, too good at fending for myself. Dad did what he could, but he was a timber carter, born in the 1920s, hardly equipped to raise a ten-year-old girl on his own. Besides, he was grieving the early loss of the love of his life too. He needed his mates and his amber anaesthesia. So, we struck a kind of unspoken accord. I made very few demands on his time, but if I wanted anything, I pretty much just had to ask. Paints for my artwork, a subscription to *Go-Set* (Australia's first pop-music newspaper), the latest clothes, a new stereo, takeaway chow mein ladled into our own pots from the new Chinese in the main street, books, records and even a prestigious and expensive seventy-two pack of Derwents. I was the envy of many of my friends, even the fact that I didn't have an ever-watchful rule-setting mum made them occasionally jealous.

Of course, none of that made up for her absence. I missed her like an asthmatic misses air, gasping for her and finding her not there. But I had no alternative, I simply had to adjust and, on the upside, my mum's early departure helped shape the independent and resilient adult I am today. On the downside (on top of losing my best friend), her loss left me with a truckload of abandonment issues that I have been grappling with ever since. A polarity that makes me at times formidable and at other times a complete wuss. Now I suspect 'loss' has a lot to answer for when it comes to how I have conducted my life since that first searing lesson. If I felt I was losing my grip on people or things I loved, it caused me to compromise or capitulate way too easily and to avoid conflict at all costs. On the flipside, the need to be good at something, 'to win' at games, at sport, in pitches, in love also made me super competitive, calling forth my formidable best. In that context, loss was a powerful positive motivator and I credit it with my big break into advertising.

In 1983, I applied for the Advertising Federation of Australia Training Scheme, where I was one of sixteen hopefuls who were shortlisted from a total of 400 applicants, with only eight to be chosen for actual positions. I remember sitting with the other fifteen in the foyer of the Clemenger Building, all of us making small talk and waiting anxiously. At the conclusion of my interview, where I sat on one side of a long shiny boardroom table being questioned by eight imposing men in suits (not a woman in sight), one from each agency offering a place, I was asked if I had anything to add. I'd been so nervous the whole way through and fumbled so many answers, that I thought I'd completely blown my chances. When asked to name a favourite ad, I couldn't even think of one, let alone my favourite. Here I was, throwing away an opportunity I'd never get again, an opportunity I knew would be a life-changer. I thought of the fifteen others in the foyer, of the confidence and the privilege I had seen on display and I could feel myself losing. Even bolstered by my brand-new Stuart Membery outfit, I wasn't going to make it unless I produced a miracle. When asked if I had anything more to say before my interview concluded, my competitive streak kicked in, and in desperation, I played to my 'disadvantage', leaving the room with this parting salvo: 'In the waiting room, I was talking to the other candidates and they all seem to have connections in advertising already—fathers, brothers, friends—so they'll get in one way or another. I don't know anyone, I'm from the country, I didn't go to a posh school, so this is my one shot.'

I was later told by the interviewer from the agency where I ended up that my 'closing comment' did the trick and moved me from the possible column, firmly into the yes column. I guess they figured that if I could sell myself so persuasively, I could sell anything, and they could use someone like me on the team. What they didn't realise was that a well-practised loser will always try harder than an expectant winner.

By the time I started high school, I was on better terms with my narrowing world. With Roy and Janine gone west, and Dad busy working at the mill or, afterwards at the pub, on his figure (expanding, not honing), I'd walk home from school, let myself in to an empty house, get a bowl of Weeties or ice-cream with Milo on top, and settle in on the couch to let TV expand my world.

I loved the American sitcoms—*Gilligan's Island*,

The Many Loves of Dobie Gillis, I Dream of Jeannie, Bewitched, Get Smart, The Brady Bunch—but I loved the ads even more. I was captivated by those little films that said so much in just thirty seconds. I wasn't yet old enough to drive a car, but if I did, I'd definitely want Amoco in my machine, because it took you up country and you got to wear cool flares and have great masses of unruly hair. I didn't like Coca Cola one bit, but thought that maybe I should try it, because apparently 'Things go better with Coke' (and I definitely wanted things to go better). Lime Fresh became our soap of choice (Lime Fresh, fresh lime) once that happy Caribbean kid with the big smile and the white teeth convinced me to try it. And the way those clever animators brought Louis the Fly to life (and death)—poor Louis—a victim of Mortein. Oh, to be able to write something that clever one day.

These ads got my creative juices flowing, and at twelve I entered a competition run by the local fire brigade. My poster and my slogan 'Fire breeds on careless deeds' won first prize and was displayed at the local fire station all summer. There was no marketing analysis to test its efficacy in the community, but the town didn't burn down that year and the success must have seeped into my subconscious.

Later, trying my hand at social commentary and in response to some bad press Kentucky Fried Chicken was experiencing at the time, I submitted this poem for a haiku exercise in year eight English:

> Colonel Sanders is in the habit
> of converting his chicken
> to Kentucky Fried Rabbit.

Miss Hirst's comment: Jo this is not really in keeping with the haiku tradition, but it is well observed and expressed nevertheless.

Many of my solitary hours in my early teens would be spent either reading or writing. Books like *The Hobbit* and *Lord of the Rings* taking me to fantastical places, *Love Story* and *The Catcher in the Rye* providing early insights into life and relationships, Agatha Christie fostering a life-long love of mystery, *National Geographic* igniting my fascination with the wider world and planting the seeds of wanderlust.

During my later high-school years, I stayed close to a small close-knit circle of friends who stood in for family, and whose families were happy to have motherless Jo stay over for nights or weekends. I particularly loved going to Hut's place because her mum was a good hearty cook. Her beef pie with homemade pastry or roast lamb with thick gravy made a nice change from Dad's standard—grilled steak and canned tomatoes with Holbrooks sauce. Or his famous 'Turkish Delight' which was not a rose-coloured dessert, but chopped-up tomato and onion in brown vinegar with his secret ingredient: half a teaspoon of sugar.

Judy Hart's mum was not a great cook, but her dad

taught us to play tennis on the new court just down the road. He was happy to hit balls at us until the sun went down, and her mum was happy to drive us all over the Yarra Valley district to play in the Section 5 Comp on Saturday afternoons, as long as we first cleaned our Dunlop Volleys with that sticky white paint.

School holidays were spent with my mum's sisters: Aunty Leila and Uncle Lance in the 'big smoke' (Box Hill) or Aunty April and Uncle Tom at their beach house in Ocean Grove. At Leila and Lance's, I had two younger girl cousins to play with, dress up with and go ten-pin bowling with. Uncle Lance had an old Holden station wagon and the treat we looked forward to most of all was going to the drive-in in our PJs, wearing towels, which we'd wrapped around our legs and rolled, so they'd sit atop our heads like Arab headdresses. Then we'd go like that to the cafeteria, pick up our tray and queue along with everyone else to make our selection from the wondrous array of cakes and sweets at the buffet. Who cared what movie was playing? This was heaven.

At Ocean Grove, my older cousins introduced me to surf culture: sunbaking, the intoxicating smell of Coppertone and the music of the Beach Boys. My cousins were like gods to me. If they invited me to play table tennis or cards with them or, better still, go to Bells Beach to watch the pro surfers from the cliff, I would almost die with delight. The day they took me to the Arab cafe in Lorne and shouted me my first iced coffee was a rite of passage I'll never forget. I thought the coffee tasted foul, saved only by the big scoop of vanilla ice-cream floating on top, but as I lounged back on the oversized floor cushions, listening to Dusty Springfield and marvelling at the exotic creatures around me, it could have been arsenic for all I cared.

At Christmas, we'd all get together for the big celebration, but my favourite time came six days later on New Year's Eve when I was allowed to stay up late and we'd all form a circle at midnight, hold hands and sing 'Auld Lang Syne', which for many years I thought was Old Lambs Eyes (and which of course has stuck to this day).

The joy of these times and the fun of being part of a big happy family made the coming home to Healesville and 'just Dad' pretty depressing. It was a jolt that I never really got used to.

Now when I think back on Col, I feel much more inclined to be generous. He may not have been the most present father, and I may not have been the most devoted daughter, but we had our moments. Mostly we found a way to stay out of each other's way, but if one needed the other, we'd always be there.

Col was a fat jolly man, think Santa sans the red suit and beard. Not the healthiest specimen you've ever seen: big drinker, pack-a-day smoker, heart attack waiting to happen. Constantly trying very haphazardly to lose weight. Reducing (pronounced 'redoosin') he called it when he stewed up some blood plums from our tree and ate them with yogurt for breakfast (his concession to healthy), followed by his usual two sloppy eggs on toast, most of which ended up down the front of his white Chesty Bond singlet. His concession to exercise was six to twelve rolls on his new gadget, the 'Gut Wheel', before heading to the pub to undo all his good work.

He had a tough gig, and when my mum first died, before Janine and Roy moved in, I asked if I could sleep with him in his bed, not understanding that it really wasn't on for a ten-year-old to sleep with their dad. (For the record, I was the kind of kid who frequently ended up in Mum and Dad's bed.) Instead, he moved my single bed into his room, pulled it up beside his half-empty double, and there it stayed until I felt brave enough to go back to my own room. I think, in truth, we were a comfort to each other.

At fifteen, I made a disastrous attempt to have sex with my eighteen-year-old boyfriend. The condom broke and I was terrified I would get pregnant (notwithstanding the fact that the penis barely got near the entry point before it exploded). Anyway, I was so scared of ending up 'stuck by misadventure' that in my panic I confessed to Dad. That alone says something about our relationship. He shed a few tears, spoke no harsh words, and just asked me to wait a couple more years before I tried again. And, secretly, I was glad to make that promise, because I really didn't want to repeat that experience. Not yet anyway.

Hot nights were a favourite time together. At sixteen stone, Col really struggled with the heat, so after dinner we often headed out to the RACV Club, which would be all but deserted, and use their swimming pool as our own. We'd take a blanket and lie on it looking up at the stars, just chewing the fat, until it was cool enough to head home. One night some city tossers approached us and said, 'You know, sir, this club is for members only.' Cool as you like, Col said, 'No problem there, mate. I'm the manager.'

For my part, I was Dad's on-call nurse and fashion advisor. As a timber worker, he often came home with log-sized splinters in his hands. They'd be deep and dirty, but nothing gave me more pleasure than digging them out with a needle (unsterilised) and triumphantly holding the offender aloft for us both to admire.

After my bed and I had returned to my own room, I would sometimes be woken in the middle of the night by a cry of anguish. I knew the source of the pain: cramp. Col suffered epic cramps in his epic-sized calves and it was my job to rush to his bedside and bend his toes back till the muscle loosened its vice-like grip. He'd be in agony and I'd do my best, but often the pressure I could muster from my five-stone mass was no match for the job, and he would writhe in pain until the cramp subsided by its own volition.

As a teenager, I would despair at his attempts to 'doll up a bit'. I know now that no kids ever think their parents look cool, but as his consultant for special occasions, I did the best I could. We'd choose the shirt with the most buttons still intact (neither of us ever thought of restitching or replacing a button), tuck it into pants that sat snugly under the pot belly, and finish with the highly polished beetle crushers. Then he'd disappear into the bathroom, where he'd part his hair on the side and slather it with Brylcreem till it stuck to his head like a helmet, all the while singing, 'A little dab'll do ya'. Somehow, women still found that attractive and despite the fact that they knew they had no chance against the memory of Olive, Col enjoyed a steady stream of would-be suitors.

We were an odd couple making the best fist of it we could: me and my teenage cynicism, him and his country-born simplicity. I judged him harshly back then for what I saw as his failings: his flagrant disregard for his health, reading the *Sun* instead of the *Age*, voting Liberal, his obsession with 3UZ, the races and *Three Way Turf Talk*, his tendency to fall asleep on the couch with a lit cigarette in his hand (which meant I had to stay awake to avert the house burning down). I often wished for a more worldly and 'conscious' father, but in hindsight I realise he had qualities I didn't credit at the time. He was funny and good company. He was generous and open hearted. Above all, he was inclusive and even quite emotionally evolved for a man of his era. He possessed no anger, he wasn't judgmental, he enjoyed the company of men and women equally. He was, as they say, just a good bloke.

When I was in grade five, the new fad at school was for girls to have autograph books, not that we ever got close to anyone famous to solicit a signature. Consequently, they were full of entries from each other along the lines of *If all the boys lived over the sea, what a good swimmer Joanne would be* or words of wisdom from selected adults, usually teachers and parents. At age ten, Col's entry meant nothing to me and I was just annoyed because with his big ugly handwriting, he had taken up a whole page of my precious book. Now it sums up the man I remember, and his take on life perfectly.

Take opportunity, for opportunity, while opportunity lasts, because opportunity, is not opportunity, when opportunity has passed.

It was late March 1979, and I'd come home from uni unexpectedly to see Dad. My visits were always haphazard and unannounced. There were no mobile phones in those days. I was on the same old green floral couch, watching the same old TV while I waited for him to come home. At about 5 pm, my brothers were driving by our house, when they saw my yellow Cortina parked in the driveway. They'd been on their way to call me from Owen's place down the road. They pulled in behind my car, came up the steps and knocked on the door. I was surprised to see them both and especially surprised to see them together. 'Brothers many,' I said, before they had a chance to speak.

Still standing on the top of the steps, they told me Dad

had died. That afternoon. On the golf course, coming up the eighteenth. He'd had a massive heart attack and dropped dead in the middle of the fairway. Heart attack waiting to happen.

So, while Olive had taken two agonisingly slow years to die, Col did it in an instant. No warning, no fanfare, no post-round pot at the nineteenth with his mates. Gone just like that. He was sixty-two and, at twenty-two, I was officially an orphan.

I reflect now that my two longest relationships with men so far have been with Col and Rex. Two more different men you wouldn't find. Col at one end of the scale, easygoing, and Rex at the other, hard work: clearly I didn't marry my father. In fact, I can only assume that my early attraction to alpha males, of which Rex was a classic example, must have been a reaction to the benign neglect dished out by Col. After the wide-open space he allowed, the freedom of that, I rebounded as far as I could the other way, seeking out the boundaries of a natural leader, someone to worship and follow, someone who'd anoint me with his charismatic blessing. Differences aside, though, there are echoes of my behaviour that were embedded with Col and that I carried over to my relationship with Rex, for better or for worse. In both cases we were just two, living alone together, mutually dependant, and I think I grew accustomed to the singularity of that unrivalled attention. I also became a default carer to them both and ultimately enjoyed the fact of them needing me as well as loving me—it was an insurance of sorts. The most striking similarity though, is how readily I was willing to accept the bad with the good. To be at times consciously critical of both men, yet able to subvert their faults in order to delight in their strengths. I simply learned to be more tolerant, more forgiving and more sticky than most, because, in both cases, I felt they were all I had.

I farewelled my family in Margaret River in time to be at Justin and Fiona's place in Aireys Inlet for my first New Year's Eve as a single. Their New Year's Eve parties were legendary, but this would be my first without Rex, so another milestone in the making. Who would kiss me at midnight? What would it be like, being the only single in this comfy world of middle-class coupledom? Would they all pity me? Would they overcompensate by trying too hard to make me feel at ease?

Hardly! By 10 pm, I was leading a chorus of girls singing 'It's Raining Men', followed by a karaoke encore of my party piece, 'Harper Valley P.T.A.' By the time midnight rolled around, I was so happy that I kissed everyone in the room out of the sheer joy of just being there and letting go.

That night, I think I experienced my first taste of the upside of being dumped. I wasn't sad, I wasn't lonely, I wasn't pining for Rex and I definitely wasn't backsliding. The film of him and Anna together—that had never left my head—started to play less often. I had only intended to stay a few nights, but I ended up staying a week. I revelled in the company of these smart, funny people; I swam in the cold ocean every morning before breakfast and felt totally Amazonian. Justin led an expedition of the willing to Eagle Rock, a large granite outcrop just off the Aireys lighthouse, me among them. Conditions were perfect for 'the jump'. High tide, no wind, sunshine, benign ocean below. As we each climbed to the ledge that matched our level of bravado, he would time the waves and call 'go' on the upswell. My turn came and the fear that naturally accompanies acts of daring like this was swallowed by the symbolism that attached to the moment. This was me letting go, jumping into the unknown, cleansing myself of the past to resurface anew.

Here with these old friends, I was not, as I feared I might be, a charity case. I was a welcome guest, maybe even more so without combustible Rex at my side. My dolphins (Eliza's term for endorphins), after many months missing at sea, returned and worked their magic on my mood and my self-esteem. To my great surprise, I found I could make people laugh and I discovered the flipside of not having Rex there to lean on was that I also didn't have to worry about his feelings or his approval. I could be 'just me' and apparently that was enough.

At night, tucked up in my cosy single bed with the sounds of the distant sea drifting through the open window, my mind would catalogue not only the events of the day, but of this whole unexpected Christmas break. *Lucky* was a word I hadn't applied to myself for a while, but it started with gentle persistence to push through, like a green shoot cracking the concrete. With it I went back to Olive, to Mum, to the good luck that had got me this far and to the bad luck that had cut her life so short.

It occurred to me that although Olive had died way too young, she had lived a 'life condensed'—forty short years, yet she made the most of them and she left a lasting impression.

Until I needed my birth certificate to apply for a passport, I'd never done the sums. When you're a child you don't think about it. When your parents are both dead, you can't ask them. When your brother has moved to the other side of the country and you're busy with the business of growing up, it doesn't occur to you to ask him either. But when you're twenty-one and about to go overseas for the first time, you stop and take stock.

My birth certificate presented some pretty startling facts. I was born on the 17th of April 1957. That much I knew already. At the time of my birth, my mother was thirty, my father thirty-eight. My brother Roy is listed as ten years old and my brother Owen as fourteen. I do the maths. That means my mum was fifteen when she got pregnant, sixteen when she had her first child. She married a man eight years her senior, when he was twenty-four and she was still sixteen. Only now with the vagaries of relationships front and centre in my mind do I begin to wonder. Was this a scandal at the time? Were my parents happy together or miserable? Was I a mistake? All these crucial things I'd never get to ask Mum or Dad, and I was running out of people who might know.

Soon after Christmas I arranged to visit Aunty Leila, mum's only living sibling (now ninety, still living in the same house in Box Hill). I took my notepad and pen and asked my many curly questions. Fortunately, Leila was still as sharp as a tack and was more than willing to talk. No, she told me, it wasn't a scandal. Ol and Col met during the war and fell in love. She and my grandmother helped Olive choose her wedding outfit. A suit and hat, not a white dress and veil, as was fitting for a war bride. She even produced photos. Yes, she was pregnant (not so unusual back then), but it was a happy marriage and they adored each other till the very end.

That was the impression I'd had through my childhood lens, but it was nice to have it confirmed. In fact, one night when we were sitting at home on the couch, I remember asking Col if he thought he would ever re-marry and he said he could never love anyone the way he loved my mum. And he never did. Though he did test-drive quite a few.

At Christmas time I'd taken the opportunity to ask Roy the question about my conception. He laughed and said: 'What do you reckon? Yes, of course you were a mistake.'

Still I'd always felt I was a well-loved mistake, so having it confirmed didn't really change anything.

All I have to go on now are my unreliable and probably embellished memories, but I still sensed that my mum was not like most mums. She wore neat slimleg pants while the other mums wore dresses. More Katherine Hepburn than Doris Day. At the beach, she wore a bright yellow two-piece bathing suit, rather than the ubiquitous and modest one-piece. There's a short memory of her that runs in my head where she is skipping along in the shallows at Ocean Grove chasing a stingray. Olive-skinned Olive: youthful, alive, incandescent in my eyes. When I replay that memory, it's always accompanied by a powerful sense of love and pride.

At our home in Healesville, before she got sick, she danced and sang all the time: 'Danny Boy', 'Somewhere Over the Rainbow', 'I'm Getting Married in the Morning'. At 11 am, we'd tune in to Swami Sarasvati on the TV and do our exercises together on the lounge-room floor. Mum had a gravitational force field that attracted everyone in her orbit. Clarrie, the local baker, always seemed to deliver our bread while Mum was sunbaking in the backyard. Alec, the butcher, always threw in free sausages with her order. When she came to pick me up from school, all my friends wanted to walk home with Mrs Peck.

Our kettle was never off the boil, with Mum's friends dropping in for a cuppa and a chat, or a Toni home perm.

I thought the sharp tang of the peroxide fumes was fair exchange for the chance to eavesdrop on their grown-up conversation. On the day I went to 'interview' Aunty Leila, she told me a story she says even she can laugh at now. When Olive died, the local shoemaker approached her and said, 'Oh Leila, what a shame it wasn't you.' And with admirable, but maybe misplaced self-effacement, she agreed.

How in the grand scheme of things can I possibly allow the conceit of feeling sorry for myself, just because life hadn't quite turned out as I'd planned, when hers had ended so painfully and prematurely. Luck is a fickle mistress whose one certainty is that you're lucky if she comes dressed to please.

After the New Year's Eve celebrations subside, all the adult guests except me drift slowly back up the Geelong Road to Melbourne, while Justin and Fiona's kids and their partners make the reverse journey to claim their time in the house of fun at Aireys.

They're not kids actually, all in their late twenties, loved up and full of life's promise, testing their first serious relationships for potential longevity. I am a fascinated observer of the dynamic of coupledom in this early phase, when the participants are not yet jaded by the triple threat of complacency, habit and itchy feet, but aided by the optimism of youth and still-raging libidos.

I am careful not to infect them with my disillusionment and cautionary tales of doom. But I am also curious about how they got together. Clearly the dating world has changed beyond recognition since my day, when you went to a pub with a loud band, drank a belly full of Stones Green Ginger Wine, spotted a spunk across the dance floor and, if you got lucky, went home for sex, after which, depending on how things panned out, you would silently grab your clothes and disappear or stay till the next morning when you'd whip up a hangover breakfast of eggs with the lot and hope for a follow-up shag—hungover, but sober this time.

As a friend of their parents, I'd watched these kids grow up, but I'd never really talked to them about 'life' until one night after a big communal dinner at the beach house, the conversation turned to dating and how they got together, and I discovered they were more than happy to share their stories.

Britt, the country cousin, and Guy met at school in Wangaratta. Their relationship, which started when they were fifteen, had withstood long separations occasioned by travel, study and the odd experiment with different partners, yet they seemed really tight. Patrick and Deanna met at the video store where she worked (Paddy confessed to borrowing way more films than he could ever watch before she finally asked him out). Megan and Ben, the youngest at twenty-six and twenty-seven, met on a dating site called Bumble—the one where girls get to make the first move.

Over the holiday break, I had been grilling the adult house guests to come up with available guys I might have a drink with, go to a movie with, test the water with. After all, these were professional people with wide-ranging and far-reaching social tentacles. Or so I thought. I was in the company of an *Age* journalist, one of Melbourne's top-rating talkback radio-show hosts, a Federal Court judge, a couple of highly esteemed educators, and an interior designer—and all their equally vibrant partners. And they were at a loss. They racked their brains, and then each offered up some lame possibility only to just as quickly discount him for reasons as diverse as they were hilarious. No, he's too set in his ways. No, he likes modelly types. No, he's still not over the woman who broke his heart fifteen years ago. No, he's not outgoing enough for you. No, he's too OCD. But my favourite response came from Sandy: 'He's okay Jo, but you can't date him, he wears Crocs—and not even ironically!'

If these well-connected people couldn't help me, things were indeed looking pretty dire. But the kids offered up another avenue: 'Try the dating apps,' they said. 'Tinder, RSVP, Bumble.' I recoiled, declaring with total certainty (and complete ignorance), that they were for fast hook-ups and young people, and that my purlieu at this delicate stage of life would be more like Silver Singles or Dinner for Eight, the thought of which horrified me even more.

Besides, having so recently and tentatively arrived at 'it's okay to be single', why was I even thinking about men? Why wasn't I content to let this new revelation rest and settle, to let the positive difference of that sink in for a bit?

It's a good question and one I weighed only briefly, because the answer, I already knew, was not that I wanted a new partner, as much as I badly wanted to prove I still had it. I wanted to avenge the humiliation of being dumped for a thirty-four-year-old, and get naked with someone new. Someone who might appreciate the care I had put into keeping my figure in shape, reboot my ego and get me over the hurdle of being unexpectedly single at sixty. And before I had a chance to register the abject superficiality of that, the opportunity presented itself.

Out of the blue, an ex-student contacted me.

Let me explain. For a short time, before I got into advertising, I was an English teacher. Or I tried to be. Mostly it was crowd control. I would get in my car, drive out to the western suburbs and attempt to teach *Romeo and Juliet* to year-nine students. On one Friday afternoon they literally disappeared out the windows. It may be an understatement to say that my grasp on discipline was a bit lacking. I put this down to two things. One, I just wasn't that into it myself. And two, I wasn't much older than the students. They just didn't take me seriously. And I didn't take me seriously either. I was an imposter, trying to act as an authority figure. I mean, I could barely remember if Juliet was a Capulet or a Montague.

My life was governed by bells and I couldn't seem to inspire or even engage my students so, in desperation, I went to see a careers-guidance counsellor who steered me towards advertising and told me about the training scheme I later applied for. I am forever grateful to her (and so should you be after hearing that someone so ill-equipped might have been teaching your kids) but my short teaching stint left me with an enormous regard for teachers. It's a really tough job and we should be so thankful that there are people out there who take it on, especially to those who do it well.

But I digress.

It seems I did make an impression on one student. His name was Dean and we had stayed in vague and very sporadic contact through a mutual friend who was principal of the school at the time. One evening while I was sitting at home alone on my orange sofa watching TV, my phone pinged—that in itself was enough to elicit a small jolt of excitement. It was a text from Dean. It had a picture of him, now probably fifty and quite a bit rounder than I remembered, but still with the naughty gleam in his eye that had him so often in trouble at school. Below that, one of Kim Jong Un, with a short message: 'Who would you choose to have dinner and a laugh with (note *with* not *at*)—top or bottom?'

Seems he'd heard about my marriage breakup then.

At the time of his text though, I didn't feel like having

dinner with anyone. My post-Christmas bravado had been swamped by an incoming tide of insecurity and 'poor me-ism' and my need for revenge had all but evaporated. It would take a lot to dislodge me from Netflix and my entrenched place on the couch. But he was persistent, and he was funny, and he seemed to understand the grieving process, having gone through a marriage breakup himself. His stupid jokes made me laugh and he had an endless supply of aphorisms that were typically trite but somehow in my reduced state made me feel better. 'Difficult roads often lead to beautiful destinations.' 'Life is too short to spend it at war with yourself.'

I responded with 'Is it a guaranteed laugh?'

'Money-back guarantee. No expectations, even better what about a movie as well? I'm partial to the Nova in Lygon Street.'

Then he followed up with a dad joke. 'How do you make holy water? You boil the hell out of it.'

So, we made a date to see a film and have a bite to eat in Carlton in two weeks time. My first Saturday-night date in decades.

Dean texted me to say he'd be at my place at about 4 pm. The movie didn't start until six, so that meant we'd have at least an hour to kill. The thought terrified me. I was totally out of practice when it came to interacting with men, and I'd seen this guy maybe twice in thirty years.

He arrived and presented me with a box of chocolates

(did people still do that?). Then we tripped over a few mountains of awkward before we found some flat ground on which to construct a conversation. We swapped stories about the ways in which our respective marriages had ended and I appreciated the fact that he was still very generous and respectful towards his ex-wife, but I guess that's easier when you're the leaver, not the one left. His two almost grown-up daughters remained a priority and were the reason he was not ready to repartner in any serious way. That came as a relief for me, removing any worry I had about where he thought this friendship might lead.

The film we saw was *Mountain*, a visually stunning documentary set to equally beautiful music, which I chose and loved, but I sensed that Dean would have been more comfortable with something starring Bruce Willis or Goldie Hawn. Over dinner, which we had at an Italian place across the road, he joked to the waitress that he was out on a Tinder date with his teacher, then he came clean and confessed to me that he actually still held a longstanding fantasy featuring his high-school English teacher Ms Peck. He recounted his memory of me in a white T-shirt (no bra), which required him to remain seated after the bell had signalled the end of the period.

I'm not sure if I found this admission flattering or embarrassing, but in my current frame of mind, it was just making me miserable. Dean was funny, as advertised, but I couldn't get past the fact that he was really just a larger, older version of the high-school larrikin I knew thirty-five years ago, and I couldn't help comparing this dinner conversation to the one Rex and I would be having if we had just seen that film together. Not Dean's fault, the film was not really up his alley, and I was still missing the ready mutuality of taste and opinion Rex and I shared in most things cultural. I know Rex would have loved that film.

After the movie, Dean drove me back to my place. He asked to come in, but I definitely wasn't in the mood for that. My discombobulation was dictating a quick, clean withdrawal, so with a chaste kiss on the cheek we said goodnight and promised to keep in touch.

That night, as I lay in my upstairs bed looking at the night sky through the clerestory windows; the fingernail moon, the flickering constellations and the infinite blackness, I realised that Christmas and the feelings that came with it was a time apart, and it would take me more than one festive season to be over Rex. Tonight had shown me that over the years his habits and expressions, his opinions and tastes, his way of being in the world had seeped deep into me, so that any others just felt foreign and unwelcome. I'd catch myself imitating a Rex gesture or saying a Rex thing and recognise the extent of the fusion that had occurred over time. At the cinema, Dean had eaten a choc-top, which scored a black mark from me simply because Rex would never have done that. Together we scorned all those people who couldn't make it through an hour and a half without a bucket of popcorn or a milkshake-sized container of Coke. If I was ever to make room for someone else in my life, I'd need to find a way to exorcise Rex and see what was left.

By the end of February, now eight months since the A-bomb, I had made some small steps forward in that regard. My apartment was a haven that I had grown to love, and I looked forward to coming home to it. I was actually enjoying cooking for one, because I could have exactly what I wanted, when I wanted it. Rex was of the opinion that soup, which I loved, wasn't a meal (especially at dinner), in fact any food that came in a bowl, except pasta, was greeted with suspicion. His specific complaint was that nothing changed from the first mouthful to the last. I would argue that if it was delicious, what did that matter? 'Boring,' he would rebut. Well, now I was dishing up a bowl of rice and veggies and seeds, pouring a glass of wine, and masochistically making my way through all five seasons of *The Affair*. This was the beginning of exorcism. It was the freedom that Francesca anticipated for me in Bali and, yes, I rather liked it.

That's not to say sadness and confusion wouldn't still launch their stealth attacks and bring me thudding back to ground zero—back to the questions I still couldn't answer. Why aren't Rex and I hiking in the Dolomites like we'd planned? Why is he living in our house with someone else? Why had he tired of me? And, of all the flavours in the shop, why had he chosen vanilla little Anna.

Terry kept reminding me that it was the bad parts of our relationship that ended our marriage. That it was natural and healthy to have fond memories of the good times and to yearn for them, but to be conscious of the darkness too. 'While you were deep in the mire of dysfunction, there was no conscious knowing of how bad the situation was.'

I accepted this on an intellectual level, but added to it with my own hypothesis, which I found more edifying. As Rex grew older, 'the special powers' he'd traded on in his youth had faded. He wasn't as attractive as he used to be and he became obsessed with ageing, complaining to me regularly that he felt old and compromised. He wasn't the vital sportsman who had been adulated at his footy and cricket clubs, and he berated his body as a traitor. He was no longer the honey pot around which the bees swarmed, and he felt their absence acutely. There was a void in his life that I could no longer fill. Rex needed that crutch of feeling special to recapture his glory days and to feel 'himself' again. So instead of turning to me, he closed me out and took his still robust charisma a'hunting. Anna with her fresh-faced youth, her doting infatuation and her willing body stepped headlong into the void.

I was mulling over this thought when, as I do every morning now, instead of snuggling up to Rex, I reached for my phone to check in with the news and the social sites, and today I see Facebook has served up a new friend suggestion.

Guess who?—Anna.

Guess where she lives?—South Melbourne (in my house).

Apparently, we have been linked because we have one friend in common.

No prizes for guessing who that is!

Bless you Mark Zuckerberg, that's the best belly laugh I've had in ages. Those algorithms are good, but it seems they lack a little in the way of backgrounding potential connections. Me and Anna friends? The suggestion is preposterous.

Though, then again, if I friended her, I could ask her all my burning questions—like how she likes my bed, I always found the memory-foam mattress really comfy, but I'd be interested in her thoughts. Or I could ask how my garden is growing? Whether the espaliered lime tree on the side wall has fruited yet? Whether she likes the bluestones in the backyard or would have preferred a timber deck? Or if that toilet in the upstairs bathroom, the one that doesn't stop flushing after you push the button, has finally been fixed.

If we became really good friends, I could ask her how she's coping with Rex's moods, if he is still given to lightning flashes of anger and maddening bouts of silence, if he's kicked his habit of tunelessly singing one line from a song over and over until murder feels like a mercy.

Ahhhh, so much to talk about. But even with the possibility of gaining all those insights, I decline to accept, though I did have a poke around her profile before I left and was delighted to find she has a grand total of eleven friends!

This could be for one of two reasons:

1. She is not that into social media.
2. She is not that popular.

Of course, I fervently want to believe it's number 2.

Naturally, I show her FB page to my friends who are wildly curious to put a face to the cause of my misery and Rex's defection.

Among the many comments I receive relating to her age, her looks, her dress sense, the weird poster in the background, this one from Eliza tickles me: 'You know, Jo, I feel kind of sorry for her. Look at her—she's a total innocent, she has no idea what she's saddled up for. Once the infatuation wears off, as it surely will, what's she left with? A grumpy old bastard with bad joints and a failing bladder.'

As if the cosmos was trying to tell me something, I'd recently found myself on the periphery of a couple of conversations where women were advocating the advantages of 'friends with benefits'.

Satisfaction without any expectation or commitment seemed to be the general gist, and because the partners are friends first, there's no awkward getting-to-know-you time and no risk of stranger danger. It's a contract without any tricky clauses.

Dean persisted and I conceded to myself that he could

be a friend, but could he be a friend with benefits? He certainly thought so, and the offer was very clearly on the table. As I weighed the possibility, I reasoned that this was probably as good a re-entry into sex as I was going to get, and I tallied the pros.

1. I was rusty and I needed the practice.
2. He was keen and uncomplicated.
3. He wasn't looking for a new partner and neither was I at this stage.
4. I could help him realise an adolescent fantasy and he could help me over what seemed like a massive hurdle.

In the con column there was really only one: I just didn't find him physically attractive.

We scheduled another date. This time we saw a movie at the Como, close to my place. A sexy Italian film loaded with suggestively slurped spaghetti and hot Roman hipsters. It was part of the Italian Film Festival, so I figured it might have an aphrodisiac effect. But Dean said it reminded him of his Italian ex-wife and did quite the opposite. How was I to know? Oh well, it was a warm Melbourne night and with skin exposed there was some incidental contact in the cinema that delivered a frisson of hope and some more deliberate touching as we sat opposite each other over dinner. We were at Ned's, where I had got to know quite a few of the waiters by name and Dean noticed that as they approached, I would pull away. 'I guess you don't really want to be seen with a guy like me in a place like this, do you?' he said. I denied it but, to my shame, it was a little bit true. Not put off by my flimsy attempt at prevarication, he then asked who my fantasy date would be if I could choose anyone, and I told him Kevin McCloud of *Grand Designs* fame. That threw him a little, but I said it was more his passionate and eloquent promotion of good design than his looks that captivated me, though I did find him quite dishy in his jeans and tweed jackets.

Back in my apartment where there were just the two of us, now with enough drinks under our belts to have dulled inhibition, I let him kiss me. And so it began, a prescribed seduction for which the script was as old as time, but the set responses, in this case, lacking the usual thrill. Later in bed with clothes removed he sensed my personal remove and told me to close my eyes and think of Kevin, which I did because the idea of sex with my ex-student Dean was sending all the wrong messages to my brain and short-circuiting any desire I was trying to muster. Here I was, naked in bed for the first time in more than twenty years with someone who was not Rex, and that was just downright weird, our movements not attuned, our steps awkward. Added to that I felt like a fraud because Dean's body was all wrong, too soft and fleshy, his skin too freckly, his lips too dry. But we'd come this far and there was no going back. For the time it took, we both managed to remain good humoured, on task and outcome-focused, and that I guess is the upside of fucking a friend. No judgment, no dashing of hopes. It was easier afterwards when we could lie back and laugh about chalking up a success for our respective missions: mine to get laid, his to finally put 'Ms Peck' to bed. But I was more than relieved when he chose not to stay the night.

Our friendship continued, the 'benefits extension' exercised one more time at his place in Dromana, then abandoned due to lack of enthusiasm on both sides. But the reconnection delivered other benefits. Dean remained available to me as an on-call counsellor and could be relied upon to cheer me up when I sank low. The other bonus, for which I was even more grateful: he'd made me curious and courageous. Dean with his unconditional positivity and barrage of compliments had given me back some belief in myself and it made me want more.

Now I was ready to test the dating apps—to put myself out there and see what I'd find.

PART 3

Experimentation

Since that fateful meeting with the careers counsellor all those years ago and my subsequent acceptance into the advertising traineeship, I've had the luxury of earning money doing something I love: writing. For most of my career as a copywriter, I've been flogging products to unsuspecting people who didn't even know they needed said products until I made them irresistible. Eliza called it the subtle art of separating people from their money.

Now I was the product. Now I was selling myself, but— to whom exactly? Desperados, sex perverts, social misfits, blokes cheating on their wives, sociopaths, voyeurs?

I was sure no self-respecting, emotionally stable, intelligent, eligible, independent, single man of a certain age would be putting himself out there on a dating site. Why would he need to? Weren't all those guys taken or, if not, then in hot demand by women much younger than me?

What's more, I was sailing into uncharted waters. I had no confidence in the process and no girlfriends I could call on to hear about their experiences. I didn't know anyone over fifty who had suffered the indignity of dating this way, let alone over sixty! But the alternatives were virtually non-existent and I was propelled by a far greater fear than humiliation. When you see two parents lowered into the ground before you turn twenty-three, you are struck by a very acute sense of the brevity and preciousness of life and, at sixty, I didn't have time to waste waiting for an uncertain future to reveal itself. I had to make my own future. My mantra became 'Won't die wondering'.

So I gathered up the tattered shreds of my self-esteem, combined them with some newly minted courage and reminded myself: I'm a writer. This is the easy bit for me. Nothing to lose. Possibly even something to gain. If not a partner, then at least an educational insight into the brave new world of online dating.

I'd been doing my research, and just about every female profile I read offered up a predictable list. It usually began with 'I enjoy' then continued with a combination of the following: movies, eating out, walks on the beach, birthdays, spending time with my family and friends, keeping fit, music, dancing, overseas travel, curling up with my cat/dog/iguana (sorry, no iguanas but I lived in hope), laughing, cooking, the occasional glass of wine, dressing up, going out. It was all so blah-blah-blah, bland-bland-bland, boring-boring-boring. Feminists would be horrified. It was all about who they were, but not about what they expected and wanted in a potential partner. It seemed a bit like putting yourself on a shelf and waiting to be picked. But then, who was I kidding, did men even read profiles? Surely, they'd be more likely to base the direction of their swipe on the photos? Putting that demoralising thought aside, I mustered my experience and this is what I wrote in my 'ad':

> Join me in my social experiment to rediscover life after 25 years of stultifying marriage. Craving intelligent conversation, spontaneity, laughs, new experiences. You'll need to be independent, funny, whip smart, fun, active and evolved. Or at least 4 out of 6.

Short, but let me tell you I sweated over those forty words more than I had over any ad I'd ever written.

I liked the idea of couching this as a 'social experiment', because that's truly what it felt like to me, and I figured if I put it in those terms instead of sounding like a dumped desperado, I might at least pique someone's interest.

I threw in the word 'stultifying' because I thought anyone who read it would at least need to know what it meant to respond. If not, they might bother to look it up. Either way it would require some nous.

Then I had to find some photos of me to put up. Which is worse than trying on bathers in a well-lit changeroom. Let me tell you, no one thinks they look good in photographs, least of all me. (Sorry, correction: no one over thirty thinks they look good in photos, not so the Instagram generation who seem to have made an artform of it.) As my back catalogue was sadly lacking, I got Eliza to snap some 'candid' shots of the 'current me' doing everyday stuff like walking nonchalantly down a street, sitting in a cafe and patting a dog, and add them to a few acceptable location shots of me on holiday, retouching Rex out where necessary.

I posted it all on Bumble and Tinder. Then started to sweat.

The photos must have been all right, but it was my list of six criteria that proved to be the real winner. It gave potentials something to 'talk about'. It gave them a way in. Amazing how many men claimed to be all six. Of course, they were discounted immediately, because they failed on the unwritten one: must not be a narcissist.

Quick lesson for those of you who are online dating greenhorns—like I was.

First, you choose your site. I chose Bumble because it requires that the woman makes the first move. That way you don't get a whole lot of men automatically swiping right and wasting your time. And I chose Tinder because it's broad and it's basic and, depending on your preference, it can be used for a quick hook-up or a proper partner search.

Then you post your profile, which requires you to set up some filters like age range, geographical proximity, where you stand on smoking, religion, relationship status and sexual preference. You can list favourite songs, films etc, but keep in mind this golden rule of advertising: don't give everything away. Keep something in reserve so you leave them wanting to know more.

One thing you are required to divulge in your profile is your age.

Suddenly I am faced with a dilemma. I have made a pact with myself for my future—no lies. But seriously, who in this cyber environment is going to type into their criteria 'seeking women sixty plus'?

IRL—in real life—women already deal with the social stigma of becoming invisible, unviable, unattractive and definitely unfuckable once they reach a certain age (unless they happen to be Helen Mirren or Lauren Hutton).

So, with the aim of getting the experiment off the ground and giving it a flimsy chance of success, I decide my birth year will serve as my age. It's only three years out and somehow fifty-seven sounds a whole lot more 'datable' than sixty.

Physically, I reckon I can pass for fifty-seven, so I modify my promise slightly and swear that, if by some crazy chance I actually meet someone I like, I will come clean immediately.

I had been warned that to enter the world of online dating

you had to 'have game'. But in my experience, you just had to *be* game. And I was. It turned out to be much more fun than I'd anticipated and I quickly became addicted.

Each morning, I'd open my apps with eager anticipation to see who was being served up to me today. You learn very quickly that the algorithms put all the best-looking men at the head of the list. The further in you get, the more you encounter singlets, stubbies, tattoos and overhanging guts. It's a rookie mistake to swipe left hoping for better to come. I did that for about a week and was later convinced I'd ditched about a hundred Mr Rights in my haste. Because once they're gone, you can't get them back. But never mind, the stocks just keep replenishing and for about every fifty you see, there are maybe five you might take a chance on, so you swipe right.

It's like standing on a pier, casting out a line and seeing if you get any bites. I'd normally do my trawling at night and then go to sleep. In the morning, I'd reach for my fishing rod (aka phone) and feel ridiculously excited to find I'd made a catch (aka match). The graphics are great too. It's like you've won the jackpot with hearts and stars bursting from your screen along with a short message to read from a complete stranger. Or in the case of Bumble, an invitation to start a discussion with Mr X.

People my age kept telling me how brave I was to tackle this, to put myself out there. They said they could never do it, would never do it, even if they found themselves single.

I was beginning to wonder, was I the weird one, or were they?

I was loving it. Suddenly the world didn't feel so empty. I was connected, but from a safe distance. I had control of the situation and I was learning a whole new vocabulary of words and abbreviations. I suppose it helped that writing came naturally to me, but I found the banter fascinating and revealing. I struck up interesting conversations with a broad range of people, including a canine dentist-come-philosopher, a Melbourne laneways tour guide, a promoter who had met Mick Jagger, and a Danish reporter working in Melbourne briefly to cover a story. As well as many suspect candidates who mysteriously did a ghostie the minute I suggested we meet. (*Ghostie,* noun. A disappearing act, where one person who has been partaking in an online conversation abruptly vanishes without trace.) I reckon they were the ones who had wives or partners and couldn't run the risk of being outed. Still, this was so much better and more targeted than the old method of cruising bars and clubs.

Most of all, I was happy with the notion of 'the experiment'. The idea, originally just a good line in my profile, was taking hold and giving me a deeper sense of purpose. The experiment was a way of monitoring my progress, mapping my recovery, fuelling my change. How many women at my age get the opportunity to do that: conduct a stocktake of life so far and then have the choice to set a new course for their future, to jump out of the life they're in and try a new one. It's probably not something you'd undertake unless circumstances dictated it, as they had in my case, but I don't think I'd be the only married woman (or man) who might have entertained the 'what if' scenario at some point in their marriage. What if I'd married X instead of Y? What if I'd pursued my dancing? What if I'd taken that job in Geneva? So, with that thought in mind, if I ever had doubts or second-guessed things, I'd counsel myself: 'Do it in the name of the experiment'. It gave me licence to try new things and to be braver than I might otherwise have been. It took me out of my comfort zone and gave me agency: I was a social scientist, this was important work, and I was really looking forward to the findings.

Establishing the criteria for evaluating the experiment's success was up to me too, so I kept it pretty simple:

- Learn more about myself
- Learn more about the world outside of marriage
- Open myself to new ideas
- Identify what's important to me in a partner now
- Prepare to kiss some frogs!

I have to start somewhere, and Franco looks like a safe first date. He has posted only one photograph. It is taken in the stands at the MCG. He is wearing a white polo shirt and shorts, very corporate looking, smiling broadly, but perhaps also a bit tentatively because he has a huge live hawk on his shoulder. I assume this was taken during the time when hawks were being employed to scare the seagulls away from the ground, but I like that Franco has chosen this one picture to sum up who he is and possibly to counter his otherwise conservative appearance. His photo says, 'Hey, look at me, I'm a man willing to mess with raptors.' His blurb informs me that he is a family man, recently divorced, ex CEO (doesn't say of what) of Italian origin and 154 centimetres tall.

The bird, the professional background and the Italianness, are enough for me to take a chance. I swipe right. Somehow, thanks to my inexperience, I don't just 'like' him, I accidentally 'super-like' him. Another rookie mistake, but what the hey, I've probably made his day. Seems so, because he 'super-likes' me right back and we start to chat. I ask him about the bird, he asks me about my work, there is nothing scintillating about our banter, but it is enough for me to assess that Franco is educated and honest, unthreatening and adequately sociable so, after about a week of chatting online, we agree to meet.

Until now I had been feeling pretty confident about meeting Franco, mainly because it didn't feel like there was too much at stake. I saw him as a way of testing my dating skills, rather than dipping my toe in the romantic water. But as soon as I crossed that line, from remote banter to designated date, the feeling changed. All the boldness I had banked in bed looking at my screen, disintegrated into doubt. And as the day creeps closer, doubt morphs into dread. Why am I doing this at all? Am I really ready to put myself out there when Rex is still so firmly fixed in my DNA?

On Thursday I become so anxious that I begin to invent reasons why I can't go: I feel a cold coming on, my week has been too stressful, there's a full moon on Friday and there'll be werewolves abroad in the city. I'm with my friend Fiona explaining these feelings to her and asking which excuse sounds most plausible when she asks to see his profile.

I hand over my phone, and she takes a squiz. The first thing she says is, 'Jo, he's 154 centimetres tall.' Being a feet and inches kind of girl, I say, 'So? What's that?' She says, 'Just over five foot!'

I hadn't bothered to do the calculation because I'd assumed that anyone who included their height in a profile would be doing so as a boast, or at least as a positive. Franco, however, was clearly doing it as forewarning.

I'm a bit ashamed to admit it, but this shifted the goalposts a little. With this new information, I could quell my fears by exacting my advantage—all six inches of it. Besides, if I pulled out now, like I was considering before Fiona set me straight, it might look like I was being heightist. But, at a tad over five foot, Franco now seemed a whole lot less intimidating. So we confirmed dinner for Friday night at the European in the city. It was his suggestion and I was more than happy with it. I hadn't eaten at a nice restaurant for ages and, if nothing else, we'd have a delicious meal.

Friday arrived, a hot one in the middle of a Melbourne summer. I probably pooed five times that day, a sure sign of nerves, but one that produced the positive side effect of leaving me with a nice flat stomach.

Getting ready, I was a mixture of cold dread and rising excitement, height advantage notwithstanding. What do you wear to meet a well-travelled ex-CEO? After a few false starts that I deemed too edgy or too casual, I decided on a simple Little Black Dress. Can't really go wrong there. I put on a bit of make-up—but not too much—and took the tram into town.

On the tram, I felt ridiculously conspicuous. I was sure that everyone was looking at me, pitying me, mocking me for my misplaced hope. But then, as I walked up Little Bourke Street in the balmy evening air, I caught a glimpse of myself in a shop window, and decided I looked okay. My stride lengthened and I was hit by an unexpected surge of happiness. All around me were groups of people, couples and after-work drinkers doing their Friday-night thing. And here was I doing a thing I'd never done before. Walking towards an assignation with a total stranger.

My old life truly was consigned to history, and this was my new normal and, to be honest, I hadn't felt this tang of anticipation in ages. In a marriage, you forego this feeling, the gut-churning thrill of dating and discovery. You trade that for security and constancy, and that's no bad thing.

But on my own, on this balmy Melbourne evening, no Rex beside me, I felt untethered, vulnerable and exhilarated all at once. On balance, I'm registering a plus. The experiment was in full swing and I was about to chart the first results.

I had contrived to be late, but Franco was later. I took the seat facing the door and waited. I pretended to be conducting important business on my phone, but I was actually busy pushing down first anxiety and then annoyance—was I being stood up on my first date? After thirty minutes, annoyance turning to anger; I wrestled with whether I should get up and go, but I'm a hardwired believer in the benefit-of-the-doubt, so I sat a little longer.

When Franco arrived soon after, looking slightly flustered, there was no mistaking him. Indeed, he was vertically challenged, but he was not unattractive. Naturally tanned in the way of most southern Italians, with a shaved scintilla of silver hair over an equally tanned pate. He dressed in the way men who are used to wearing suits do when they are attempting casual. A casual so tortured the effect is anything but. Pressed pale chinos, blue check shirt with button-down collar, boat shoes that have never seen a deck and, in this heat, a completely superfluous navy linen jacket. He had clearly chosen this place because he was a regular—he was greeted and feted at the door, and shown to our table amid much fanfare, prompting the obvious opener from me, 'You come here often?'

Unfortunately for him, this show of status, clearly

orchestrated to impress, had the opposite effect on me. But, I noted with relief, he was nervous too. His lateness was explained away by a missed train, which I not only accepted, but awarded him points for, pleased that he was not above taking public transport.

It's a general rule of online dating that you keep the first date short, limiting it to coffee or a drink, in order to allow one or the other to beat a hasty retreat if it's a disaster. As we're handed the menus, which are the size of small encyclopaedias, I remind myself of this and wonder why I said yes to a commitment that would surely leach into a second hour.

We place our orders, which is another challenge when familiarity is missing: do we have entrees, do we share, does he prefer white or red, will I get the bread roll and give it to him as I always did with Rex? But with those hurdles crossed we settle into conversation and I learn that Franco is Sicilian and, since retiring as CEO of an accounting firm, he has taken his passion for karate to the next level, now coaching professionally and touring with his Olympic hopefuls. Plenty to talk about there, and no trouble filling the time, but there's no side serve of frisson, and I have already determined that this is not going beyond one date. Not so Franco. He's already planning our first trip together and fast-forwarding to me loving his big extended family when I meet them.

One of my skills, developed over years in my people-facing

business, is that I know how to make myself likeable. This involves asking questions, listening to the answers, sometimes overdoing the interest, and remaining a mystery myself. One of my drawbacks is that I'm not very good at being critical or direct. I'm a conflict-avoider, remember.

My instincts about Franco were spot on. He was indeed a genial and safe first date, but on the footpath outside, I am faced with the prospect of delivering my first let-down. How to be honest but not hurtful? Damnably contrary Melbourne is conspiring to make this even harder for me, turning on a night that is the very essence of romantic. A warm breeze plays in the plane trees above, Parliament House glows, waiters shoosh around pavement tables serving lovers who laugh and look meaningfully into each other's eyes.

Franco is waiting and his expectation is palpable. I'd had a truly enjoyable night so I launch with that, but what I can't bring myself to say is that for me there is zero chemistry and that this couldn't possibly go anywhere, especially to the places he is imagining. So instead, I fall back on something that's plausible and partly true. I say I am too freshly out of a thirty-year relationship to entertain another one just yet. I hadn't banked on it being so confronting. I have probably gone public too soon. I hope he understands.

Franco is a gentleman. He says of course he understands, then offers to take me home in a taxi. He sits in the front seat with the driver and the two of them spend the entire trip discussing the relative merits of Bitcoin. When we pull up at my driveway he gets out of the cab, opens my door, thanks me for a lovely evening and shakes my hand. Total class.

When you are part of a couple for so long, your world tends to narrow. Rex and I consciously railed against that containment with our travel and adventures, but outside of those, pressured by the routines and stresses of a busy work life, it was inevitable that complacency would creep in. We'd see the same circle of friends; revisit favourite places to holiday, eat, see a film; our daily walks would follow the same few paths; and even the way we had sex (when that was still happening) became a well-practised dance. You come to know each other so intimately, your rituals so ingrained, that you simply fall back on familiar patterns, because they are comfortable and reliable and 'nice'.

What I was liking about my new circumstances was that if I wanted 'a life' I had no choice. I simply had to get off the couch, as comfy as it was, and try new things. And if I wanted a relationship, I needed to meet new men and to do that I had to keep fishing.

Before we even meet, Alex sends me a link to an Amy Schumer video called 'The Museum of Boyfriend Wardrobe Atrocities'. Google it and you'll see why I was so excited to meet him. Alex was date number two and I had high hopes for any man who would pick that out, find it hilarious and read me well enough through a series of texts to know that I would too.

On top of that, he chooses Leonard's House of Love as our meeting place—just for the irony. Ohhh, this is looking good. We joke that it might turn out to be Leonard's House of Long Silences, Leonard's House of Awkward First Dates, or Leonard's House of Thank God There's Alcohol. In reality, it turns out to be Leonard's House of the Vapid, Vain and Vacuous who don't want us there ruining their Instagram shots. And, as we don't want to be there feeling like dinosaurs, after one drink—which was long enough to establish that we both loved dumplings—we go off in search of some.

Whether he's nervous or just out of touch, Alex simply can't or won't make eye contact with me. I feel my bubble deflating before the second plate of dumplings arrives. So much anticipation, sapped by a simple failing. I let him tell me all about himself while he's looking somewhere off into the middle distance over my left shoulder. Member of a daggy dad band. Separated with two kids. Contestant on *Rockwiz*, got to kiss Julia Zemiro. He really doesn't draw breath long enough to ask me anything about myself and, when he finally does, he doesn't wait for the answer. But my sense is that Alex is not fuelled by ego, more at the mercy of nerves, so I pull out my old benefit-of-the-doubt persona and persevere.

I like Alex, he's got layers. On top, he's a newly minted bachelor who has not yet learned how to make an impression. His clothes are too big and mismatched as if thrown on in a hurry, which is probably true since he had to feed his kids before he made his way across town to meet me. And he has that slightly musty smell that drifts alongside men who are not too familiar with the washing machine. But under that he is funny and quick-witted with an impressive grasp of popular culture, which he demonstrates by googling a hilarious American ad for period products featuring Aunt Flo. When he asks me to guess his profession, I take a stab at journalist. He takes that as a compliment, but concedes his job in IT is much less interesting.

Then into the conversation he launches a curve ball, confessing he is a recent cancer survivor. I know that took courage to say, but it immediately reframes our date and puts me on less-solid ground. I had already decided Alex was not for me, and I was preparing my getaway speech, but in this grey space does compassion alone dictate a second chance? To avoid the conversation that is now imminent, and to buy time to think about how I feel, I short-circuit our goodbye, telling him outside the restaurant that I am tired and suggesting that he head straight to the station which is just up the road. Then I stand there like a stiff budgie while he embraces me and kisses me goodnight.

Before my head hits the pillow, there's a text from him saying what a great night he had. I don't answer until the next morning because I feel quite conflicted about Alex. Here's a guy who's emerging from a breakup and a brush with death, brave enough to date, although not yet nailing eye contact, but genuinely funny and totally devoid of pretence. He'd make a great friend, but I know he's not looking for a friend, and neither am I. So why is Alex out? It's those damnable first impressions that refuse to be ignored and simply won't bargain with compassion or potential. I wish I was a better person, I wish I could look beyond the wrapping, but for all the personality in the world, if you can't imagine jumping someone's bones, there's really no point progressing. In the morning, I tell him in the nicest way I can that I'm just not feeling it, that for me there was no chemistry. He probably senses the lie behind that, because he ghosts me immediately and all our texts are wiped. That stings, because I know he is hurt, but also because I really wanted to keep a record of all our fabulous banter.

I know I have turned a corner when I show up at Terry's office and the tissues have been put away. She asks me how I am, and I answer with an unqualified 'Great!' Instead of Rex and my precarious state of mind, we talk about work, dating and my new apartment. In the dark days, I was seeing Terry every week, and I needed those visits as much as I needed oxygen. After about two months, we switched to fortnightly check-ins, which were still necessary as I tried to make sense of what had happened and why, reverting to 'What could I have done differently?' Terry would patiently and professionally pull me back from the guilt precipice and remind me that I was a player in the separation but not the key shot-maker.

Today, it almost feels like we are filling in time, and it's a good sign that in the back of my mind I am thinking this money could be better spent on a lamp I saw at Grandfather's Axe or, better still, a writing course. While I am thinking it, Terry calls it.

She says, 'Jo, I'll always be here if you need me, but for now, I think you're good to go.'

As I leave her office for what might be the last time, I acknowledge that I am a lighter person. All the weight that pressed in on me during my marriage has been lifted. It's incredible to think about how much time and energy was wasted just maintaining a liveable harmony. The contortions I performed to keep us together.

Part-way through our sessions, Terry had predicted that once my head was clear, I'd be amazed by how much space would be freed up for positive thought. And she was right—I'm beginning to feel my creativity kick in again. I have room for happiness and inspiration and indulgent flights of fancy. I have the bones of this book taking shape in my mind and I lie awake at night letting the ideas flood in, instead of trying to keep the past out.

That night I pick up a book that has been recommended

to me by Genevieve. It has been on my bedside table for a while, overlooked in favour of trashier, easier reads. I flick through the first few pages to see if I think it's the right book for me now, when I come across this quote from Marcel Proust's *In Search of Lost Time* in the foreword:

> Ideas come to us as the successors of griefs, and griefs, at the moment they turn into ideas, lose some part of their power to injure the heart.

I'd call that a resounding 'Yes' from the cosmos, and I devour *Shell* by Kristina Olsson with a mixture of admiration and envy.

Owen, date number three, won't take up much of your time, because he didn't take up much of mine. We matched because we work in related fields. He's an advertising photographer and I thought that might make him interesting, at least creative, and give us something to talk about. But the warning signs were already flashing when he cancelled our two first dates. I told him, by text, three strikes and you're out, so at least he managed to show up the third time. Now I'm wishing he hadn't, for a blander man you'd never meet. It's revealing that I can barely remember a specific detail about him, except that he was small. Not just small of stature, but uncommanding in every way. His conversation was dull and laboured and I found myself thinking about the deadline I was jeopardising just to be here, wishing I was back at my desk finishing the task. I asked him about his photography. Still life. Just as well, I thought, because I couldn't imagine this man inspiring a model to bring out her/his best. As I sat there feigning interest in his family but understanding implicitly why his wife left him, that quote from Oscar Wilde popped into my head. 'There are two kinds of people in the world—those who make you feel better when they enter the room, and those who make you feel better when they leave.'

I got the feeling I'd always be waiting for Owen to leave and perhaps his wife had too, until he didn't and she had to take matters into her own hands. This time, luckily, I'd had the good sense to schedule a short daytime coffee date, so with lattes and prospects of love empty, we got up and went our separate ways.

So here I am, three dates down, and even though I haven't struck gold (or even silver or bronze), I am not yet put off by the process either. In fact, like anything else in life, it gets easier with practice. The biggest surprise is that you can and do find interesting men online. Men who are looking for love and connection. And age is no barrier to entry. My initial fear that online dating was strictly the province of the young has been totally turned on its head.

When Rex and I first split, Francie said to me that she felt it was an especially cruel time to be abandoned—she was referring to my age. At the time, I agreed with her. My life's plans were in disarray. My life's work felt pointless (without the person I planned to spend the spoils with).

And I was staring down the barrel of ageing alone.

I'm now pleased to say that view has changed. At sixty, you've actually got a lot of ticks in the positive column. For starters you've mostly been through your mills. You've done the hard yards with work, family and empire-building. If you're like me, you may even experience an impulse to simplify, and to prioritise personal development and benevolence over status and the accumulation of stuff. These days I'd much rather go to a yoga class and work on my internal connections than buy jewellery to impress my external ones. Age bestows a confidence, which comes with a liberating hang-the-consequences attitude. When you're young, you worry and censor endlessly because everything matters so much. Now I'm beginning to appreciate the freedom and reward that comes with living out loud and caring less. When Eliza asked me recently what I really thought of the man she was living with, I answered honestly that I felt he was no match for her boisterous vibrancy, that his Swiss precision seemed the antithesis of her Irish naughtiness and that since she had been with him, she had seemed pricked by his judgment and censure. All the air gone out of her. Maybe I wouldn't have been quite so truthful if she wasn't already germinating the same thoughts herself, but I know that because I didn't sugar-coat my response, she took notice and later found the courage to leave him.

In fact, just as they say 'youth is wasted on the young', I'm starting to think 'age is wasted on the old'. I'm not talking here about the aches and pains that bid you good morning most days, or the saggy skin that refuses to bounce back, or even the extra kilos that no diet seems to budge. What I am talking about is the wisdom and licence that comes with maturity. Your right to dispense with niceties: don't like your new haircut—tell your hairdresser, there's nothing to be gained by protecting their feelings. Exercise your permission to say no: if you really don't want to go to that funeral, then don't. The dead won't judge you and if the living do, that's their problem. Revel in your resolve to remove the filters that keep everything 'acceptable'. I would have loved a bit of that latitude to kick in earlier, say in my forties or fifties, when sucking up seemed to be a necessary survival skill, especially in advertising, where the client was always right even when they were patently wrong. That was a very difficult accommodation for me and I never really got used to it.

And then political correctness kicked in and spoilt all our fun even more. I was always being told, 'Jo, you can't say that,' when all I was doing was speaking the truth. 'Sorry, I don't think I can work with you.' 'He's okay, but I reckon you can do better.' 'Yes, your bum looks big in that, but that's because you have a big bum. Instead of agonising over it, learn to love it. As far as I can tell, Kim Kardashian made a motza off the back of her arse.'

Well, now I can, and I do. And guess what? You'd be surprised how many people find it refreshing to be told something straight. Clarity is good for everyone. Good for the teller, good for the receiver. It leaves no room for misinterpretation. For instance, I love a good social get-together, but I am not a long sitter or a late stayer. When the time comes—my cut-off time—I have no qualms about standing up and saying, 'Thanks, that was a wonderful evening, but I've had enough now, wouldn't want to spoil a good thing.' Or, when dealing with dinner guests who look like outstaying their welcome, I have been known to say, 'Okay, you freeloaders, time to fuck off now, I need to go to bed.'

So, while my mental state was looking up, my love life remained a work in progress. Victor and I didn't actually make it to a face-to-face date, but I'm including him in the story for a couple of reasons: he provides a cautionary tale and you'll get a better idea of what Tinder banter can look like.

You can make up your own mind whether I missed out on a great opportunity or dodged a bullet.

> **MON 19 FEB**
> Hi Victor
> On paper (or should I say on screen) we seem
> like a great match. I'm also a writer, I share
> lots of your interests and I'm a sucker for
> anything or anyone European.
>
> > Hi Jo
> > Without wishing to brag, I grew up in
> > Melbourne as a wog and score 6 out of 6 on

your essential criteria. I also consider lack of
passion and creativity as deal-breakers. I try
to learn something new from everyone I meet
and like to find partners in crime.

SAT 24 FEB

Hi Jo
It's a nice change when a woman makes the
first move. Hope it wasn't your last.

Hey Victor
Can't make up my mind about you. I really
liked your profile, then I decided your ego
might be too big an obstacle to negotiate.

Hi Jo
Reading back my first message where I was
trying to be a bit funny, I can totally see how
you might think I must be a full-on narcissist. As a writer, you've no doubt scrawled
things out (and maybe even sent them off)
before realising you've got the tone all wrong.
There's no guarantee. But a drink is surely a
low-risk investment to learn who or what lies
behind the masquerade.

Hi Victor,
Yes, I am familiar with that pitfall. So,
in the spirit of being open with my social
experiment, I'm prepared to suspend
judgment till we meet. Happy to have a drink
as long as it's obligation-free and we are
prepared to be totally honest.

> Hi Jo
> I also wouldn't want it any other way.

TUE 27 FEB

Victor
We seem to have stalled. I am at Coda having
dinner with a friend and she says I have to
meet you. So, what about it?

WED 28 FEB

> Sorry Jo
> I only just read this. Happy to meet
> tomorrow eve if that suits you. How come
> your friend is so emphatic?

She is not as hard a judge as I am and she
wants to know how you ended up in a photo
with Mick Jagger.

> The encounter with Mick, Keith and Ron
> was during BBC filming and recording for the
> *Continental Drift* album in Tangiers in 1990.
> Are you a Stones fan? If you can't do a brief
> encounter Thursday afternoon or early eve,
> let me know when's good for you next week.
> I'm in Thornbury. And you?

THU 1 MARCH

> South Yarra. And yes, I'm a massive Stones
> fan. I was at their first Australian concert at
> Kooyong all those years ago.

I was at that same Kooyong gig. I also had a poster of that Annie Liebowitz photo of Mick on stage where he exudes his ravenous libido. Many years later, I interviewed Mick Taylor and Bill Wyman. Sadly, both pretty miserable sods. Can we check in on Tuesday to agree which day is best to meet?

FRI 2 MARCH

You've obviously had a full and interesting life. Lots to talk about when we meet—have a good weekend.

MON 5 MARCH

> Hi Jo
> Hope you've had a rousing kickstart to your week. Just to say that Thursday eve is going to be best for me. Is that okay for you? When do you finish work? We can meet either near your work or close to your place if you prefer to go home first. You choose.

THUR 8 MARCH

Hi Victor
Are you still up for that date tonight? If so, I thought we could meet at L'Hotel Gitan in Prahran around 6.30. If not, we can raincheck for another time.

SUN 11 MARCH

What happened?

WED 14 MARCH

> Jo, my tinder account crashed and had to get replacement UK SIM card sent express in order to log back in using UK number. I've been very busy recording demo songs for my musical project. In studio today to Friday then have to fly to London on Sunday. Fate was not working for us. Can I call you around 6 pm this eve?

> Well Victor, at least you didn't get hit by a bus or have a heart attack. Just a couple of my more generous theories. Anyway, you sound busy, so why don't you check in when you get back from London, if there's any real interest…

And that was the last I heard of Victor.

It didn't take me long to come down on the side of 'bullet dodged'. But even now when I reread those texts, pompous as they sound, I kind of wish I had met Victor just once. To reconcile a man who uses terms like 'eve' and 'sod' and 'rousing kickstart' with someone who has interviewed Bill Wyman and Mick Taylor. And I know he really did because he sent me the link. So, while my prospects of finding love online were yet to register so much as a blip, I have to admit the opportunity to parry like that with a person in cyberspace still fascinated me. The experiment and the criteria I set for investigation were delivering insights, if not actual possibilities: I was learning more about myself, I was learning more about the world outside of marriage, and I was enjoying the process of opening myself to new ideas and people.

Rudy is my first lesson in spontaneity.

I'm home in my PJs on a Saturday night watching my favourite guilty show, *Death in Paradise*. It's not terribly demanding viewing, so I'm having no trouble following the plot while also flicking through the latest suggestions from Bumble when I see Rudy.

He has longish grey hair, a face writ large with life, a series of shots that show him at a wedding, on a boat, in a Japanese restaurant, skiing somewhere that didn't look like Australia and a profile that includes, among other things, 'Good EI'.

Another initialism I have to look up. Turns out EI stands for emotional intelligence.

I'm always suspicious of people who feel the need to say these things, because often the exact opposite is the case, but there's something about Rudy that seems genuine, so I swipe right—and instant exploding graphics precede the pulsating word MATCH!

That means he'd already 'liked' me so, this being Bumble, it's up to me to start a conversation. Without giving it much thought, I say something terribly original like 'Hi Rudy, what you doing?' not expecting him to actually be home on a Saturday night. But that's the thing about online dating. If they're there, you're live.

The banter begins and it's good enough to distract me from the big reveal on *Death in Paradise*. I learn that Rudy lives in St Kilda and is something of a jack-of-all-trades. Ex-mechanic, motorbike enthusiast, passionate skier, now dabbling in many things including a winter job in the mountains, where he cooks and does maintenance for a friend at her ski lodge, and gets to ski all season long. At home he's a regular contributor to the St Kilda community garden project. That's quite a grab bag of good stuff so I progress to 'Should we meet sometime?'

He says, 'Yeah, what about now?'

My desire for spontaneity is being put to the test. But I'm already a few wines in, and I had promised myself an early night. I say as much and he says, 'Okies, Jo—sleep well.'

Okies is another new term for me, but I immediately like it and I like Rudy too. There's something easygoing and promising about him. And a distinct lack of pressure.

The next day I'm playing golf with Fiona. I play badly, and golf always reminds me of Rex. Of the good times. So by the time I get home I'm in a bit of a funk.

I decide to contact Rudy and ask if the offer still stands.

Again, he gets straight back: 'Yes, but only until tomorrow night. Tuesday morning I'm off to Falls Creek. It's a lovely day, let's meet now for an afternoon drink.'

I have Samantha coming for dinner, but I don't want to say no again. So I agree to meet him at a bar he suggests in Windsor, knowing that my dinner plans will give me an excuse to get away.

I'm cruising slowly up Chapel Street in my car looking at the numbers when I spot the bar and, as luck would have it, a park right out front. It's a tight spot which requires a precision parallel park, then as I indicate to pull in and turn my head over my right shoulder, I feel eyes on me. There's a man sitting on a high stool at a footpath table, he is watching me and smiling. Miraculously I don't fuck the parking up and as I get out of the car, he raises his half-full glass to me.

As we smile and acknowledge each other, I take the stool opposite and order myself a glass of riesling. The five-second test has already put Rudy in the 'possible' category. That assessment is based on nothing more substantial than looks: craggy face, long grey hair swept back off his forehead, not fat, old jeans, weathered cotton shirt with the sleeves rolled up. And he's drinking white wine.

We talk easily and I discover he's of Dutch descent, twice divorced with a couple of grown-up children living interstate. Still on good terms with both his ex-wives. After more getting-to-know-you conversation, he tells me he's now in an 'open relationship'.

'Okay,' I say, 'tell me about that.'

He and Mimi, his partner, live together but have an

agreement that they can see other people.

'Okay—how does that work?'

I am more curious than shocked by this and I immediately want to know more. Mostly I want to know if people who profess to have this kind of arrangement can actually make it work—without jealousy or recrimination. Do they discuss their other partners, and how do they guard against getting emotionally involved?

I fire my questions and he is more than happy to oblige. He says it started a few years ago when Mimi was going to France for the first time on a work trip. Before leaving he gave her 'permission' to explore all possibilities and opportunities, even if that included other men. Then, on a visit to the Opera Garnier, she met an Italian man during interval, also in Paris for a short time, and after the performance went back to his hotel. She told Rudy everything and still now catches up with her Italian lover whenever their schedules happen to coincide.

It's such a romantic story, which quite possibly is total bullshit, but the way Rudy relates it, it feels authentic. Regardless, I want to believe. And more than anything, I want to be Mimi and have that experience for myself. At the same time, my respect for Rudy's EI is growing.

I am finding this conversation and this man fascinating, but time is running out and I really need to get home and start dinner before Samantha arrives. The thing is I'm not done with Rudy and the feeling is mutual. Today is Sunday, he is leaving town on Tuesday, so it has to be tomorrow night or wait another two months, by which time the moment will surely have passed.

As we part, I write my address on his hand and say I'll see him tomorrow around seven. There was no pretence that he was simply coming for dinner—we had talked openly about sex. I told him about Dean, the pragmatic nature of that arrangement, and confessed that I had not experienced great sex for such a long time, even when I was with Rex, that I feared I may have lost the knack or perhaps used up my life's quota. Inherent in that admission is a considerable load of pressure, but Rudy promised to be a considerate and respectful lover.

Aside from that, we liked each other. Conversation had come naturally to us and during its course Rudy had mentioned that he wasn't simply seeking a one-night stand, but a semi-permanent second lover. And the more I thought about it, the idea of a 'no strings' relationship with a man I found easy company kind of appealed to me too. I certainly wasn't ready for commitment. But company? Yes. Connection? Yes. Diversion? Yes.

The experiment was teaching me a lot about the nuance contained within the word *relationship*. I realised that the constraints of marriage and monogamy were necessary for some, but totally unrealistic for others. I liked the idea that there could be other possibilities. Forty-five years ago, when I was back on that post-and-rail fence with my friend Hut, and before I confined myself to the terms of my marriage contract with Rex, I'm sure I had a broader view. But in order to make my marriage work, I banished those impulses. Now I was meeting all sorts of people who had other ideas and seemingly made relationships work in various non-traditional ways.

Samantha was a timely friend to have in my arsenal in that regard. As we slurp our way through a huge pot of garlicky tomatoey mussels (was there ever a more delicious throw-together meal?), she gets the full download on Rudy and gives me the unequivocal thumbs up on the plan. While my long-term friends might have been more likely to err on the side of caution, she visibly fizzes with excitement on my behalf. She hugs me and high fives me for my speedy recovery from marriage mortality and my willingness to put myself out there. Her only regard for me personally is that I put Rex completely out of my head, cast the arbitrary notion of my age aside and have fun.

My biggest shock comes when the doorbell rings the next evening and I open it to a giant. Rudy is all of six foot seven. It occurs to me that he hadn't actually stood up yesterday, so this is a surprise. I remember reading that the Dutch were the tallest people on the planet and here was living proof. A long lean Dutchman bearing a backpack, out of which comes a bottle of white wine and some contributions to our indoor picnic.

Then his phone rings. Mimi. There's no embarrassment,

no trying to cover and clearly no questions from her that require veiled answers from him. It seems a very normal conversation that any couple might have and it ends with, 'Okies, see you later.'

Something about Rudy makes me feel totally relaxed. I'm under no pressure to impress. If he doesn't like me, it doesn't matter because he has someone else to fall back on. If I don't like him, I can rationalise that he wasn't really available anyway. We're not placing a whole lot of expectations on each other. Added to that, my bullshit detector is not picking up any worrying signals. I place a low ottoman in front of the orange couch and spread out our picnic goodies on it. I've bought dolmades, octopus, tarama, olives and crusty bread. He produces some shop-bought salads and a bottle of chardonnay. Already we are combining well. As we eat, drink, talk and find each other's feet on the ottoman, the evening morphs seamlessly from one thing to another.

Upstairs, the backpack reveals more surprises: a music player loaded with unfamiliar tracks—jazz and blues, which transform my bedroom into a moody Amsterdam nightclub—and some exotic body oil, the woody scent of which stays with me for weeks after.

We sit on the edge of the bed and Rudy asks if he can undress me. I wasn't sure what to expect, but I'm gratified that this isn't to be one of those frantic 'fuck me now' scenarios, but a languid and deliberate journey guided by sensuality and exploration. As my garments are slowly peeled away, I feel the opposite of naked. I feel clothed in a memory of confidence and charged by the fizz of anticipation.

In my experience, when it comes to cunnilingus men fall roughly into three categories:

1. Those who will never go there.
2. Those who know they should go there and do so, badly.
3. Those who love going there and have it down to a fine art.

With Rudy, I hit the jackpot.

As soon as his long grey hair brushes the tops of my thighs, I feel the beginning of something. Something like a wave, far out on the horizon, starting to swell. I am relaxed and patient as it draws slowly closer; forming, shaping, curling, teetering for delicious seconds between the making and the breaking. Finally, with the weight of the water, it collapses rolling, rolling, rolling until it dissipates into a layer of effervescing skin-tingling seafoam.

Not one perfect wave. But two.

Around midnight, Rudy repacks his backpack and lets himself out, leaving me with the imprint of something deeply felt and long lost.

Rex and I split in June 2017. It's now March 2018.

This date marks an important threshold. Behind me is my old life, my old thinking. Ahead is a future waiting to be formed.

The devastation that delivered me here was not something I would ever have signed up for, even with the benefit of a crystal ball. But I can say now, unequivocally, that I am in a better place. For starters, I am no longer living on high alert. My anxiety has subsided. The white noise of constant worry has been silenced. My wrinkle accumulation has slowed. The need to please has been replaced by the wonderfully emancipatory 'please myself'. Small things deliver huge pleasure. If I stay in bed until midday, no one knows. If I don't have a shower for two days, no one cares. If I want wine and chips for dinner, that's my choice. The freedom of having no one to answer to is intoxicating. When I close the door to go to work, I know I'll find the apartment exactly as I left it when I come home. There's no negotiation about what to watch on TV, what I can buy, where I can go or when.

Plus, there's the promise of Rudy coming back, plenty of invitations from friends to fulfil my need for social contact, and the immense and newly discovered joy of going to a movie alone.

Dating apps should come with a warning. They are seriously addictive.

So, even though I'm loving my new-found independence and am happy with the Rudy solution for the time being, I can't quit my nightly fix.

I go to bed, read a few chapters of my book, and wrestle with whether to pick up my phone before I go to sleep.

The phone always wins. Call it FOMO. Or PHONE-MO.

> Peter 59—left
> Corey 62 (hmmm architect, maybe)—right
> Phillip 102—definitely left
> Davo 65—left
> Warren 54 (hmmm, cute)—right
> Gavin 67—left
> Rusty 52—left
> Frank 57—left

Getting tired now.

> Richard 58—left
> Five more then I'll stop
> Ray 63—left
> Steve 50—left
> Magnus No age—left
> Michael 52—left
> Paul 50—left
> Goodnight, my would-be lovers.

In the morning, I have a match with Warren.

Who was he again? When I check, there is something about his picture that's appealing, along with his caption:

'Windswept and Interesting'.

Below that just two facts: Tailor. Like making things.

Not much to go on. I put it out of my mind and go to work.

Turns out Warren's real name is Edwin.

Early text exchanges confirm he is actually a tailor, online he is Warren, after the Dave Graney song Warren Oates, and his spelling is woeful.

But he intrigued and hooked me—an ex-English teacher and copywriter—by using a word I'd never heard before.

I mention to Edwin that it's taking me ages to decipher his bad spelling and grammar, and he blames his big clumsy hands. I suggest that the big hands might be the result of all that 'sewing and making' he does. He replies, 'Shame on you for your Lamarckism.'

At first, I think it's another of his spelling mistakes. The cap 'L' seems random and out of place, while 'a-r-c-k' is definitely not a usual letter sequence—but before I accuse Edwin of more crimes against the English language, and in order not to make a fool of myself, I look it up.

Good thing I did. Lamarck was a French naturalist who developed an early theory of biological evolution postulating that 'an organism can pass on to its offspring physical characteristics that the parent organism acquired through use or disuse during its lifetime'. The article cites the example of giraffes whose necks have become longer by stretching to reach foliage, passing this change down to their young.

It turns out Lamarck's theories of acquired characteristics have since been debunked but, give the fellow credit, he predated Darwin and his were among the earliest recorded theories of evolution of the species.

I'm more than a little fascinated by a tailor who is familiar with Lamarck and his theories and refers to him during casual banter on a dating site. Especially one who claimed to meet only four of my six criteria, the two misses being 'smart' and 'funny'. With self-deprecation like that on show, I resolve that I have to meet Edwin.

Five nights later, a Sunday, I struggle up the steep wooden stairs at the Neighbourhood Wine Room, cursing the platform slides I have chosen to make my legs look longer, and glance across to the bar where a man is sitting. He is the only single man there, so it has to be him. I stop to take him in, and in those few seconds before we are revealed to each other, my confidence dissolves. It's replaced by a churn that I know will blank my personality, because I sense it already—this one might matter.

I notice clothes. Always have. At home I agonised over what to wear to meet a tailor and now I wish I'd tried a bit harder than baggy boyfriend jeans, old Gorman tee and height-enhancing slides. My reasoning was that this uniform of contemporary acceptance, although unlikely to impress, could do no harm either, except, belatedly I realise, to make me look totally unimaginative. Because now I'm looking at a tall slim man who knows, unlike Franco, exactly how to nail casual. He's wearing a maroon short-sleeved shirt with a small beige spot print. It's tucked into a well-worn pair of grey check pants that are rolled at the hem so his ankles are showing. Beautiful sinewy ankles. His feet, resting on the bar stool, are shod in old-school leather sandals like the kind you see on villagers in Greece. There's a well-worn raffia hat on the bar, and he's drinking a glass of rosé. At that moment he turns towards the door. I wave acknowledgment that I'm his date, and his face, serene and kind in a slack puppy-dog kind of way, compounds my discombobulation.

As I approach the bar, I manage something like, 'Hi, I'm Jo.' 'Edwin,' he says and puts out his hand which I inexplicably bypass, kissing him awkwardly on the cheek.

'Oh, going there already?' he says, which causes me to blush like a teenager and wish for a chance to restart the whole thing.

To help things move on, he hands me the wine list and asks what I'd like to drink, but the printed words won't stay still. I can't focus, can't even remember what I like, so I ask what he's having. He points to a listing under the heading 'Skin Contact'. Seriously? 'Skin contact'? Were the gods having a joke with me? I'd never seen that term on a wine list before and I had no idea what it meant except for the image it was creating in my brain, so I say, 'I'll have one of those'.

For the record, this is not something I would ever do. It's one of my pet hates: people who don't rate the enjoyment of eating and drinking highly enough to know their own taste and make their own choice. But here I am, aged sixty, perched precariously on a stool, displaying all the symptoms of a teenage crush. For the first half hour, I'm sure I make no sense. I can't concentrate on what he's saying because I'm already worried about what I should say next. My mind is either racing ahead or a total blank.

About an hour has passed in stilted discussion before we stray into past-relationship territory and Edwin drops this revelatory tidbit: 'Actually, I've just escaped a six-year relationship with a woman who became progressively more and more controlling. It took me three years to recognise it and another three to find my way out.' On hearing that, my focus returns with interest. For starters, and for some inexplicable reason, I hadn't considered the idea that this partnership dynamic might be reversed, with women doing the controlling and men doing the tap-dancing. I wanted to know all about that, how his experience might compare to mine, and for that to happen I needed to be present and receiving.

We decide to move from the bar to a table, and while Edwin is in the bathroom, my composure is restored enough for me to order some small plates; half a dozen oysters (which I get to eat all of because Edwin is an oyster denier), an eggplant-and-pepper salad, some aged prosciutto with ciabatta and some fat chips with aioli, which turns out are his gustatory addiction.

On this occasion we talk only briefly about our former partners, not wanting to bring too much of a downer to our unresolved date. What emerges even from our initial chat is that Edwin and I have had similar experiences living with precarious people. Negotiating the unpredictability of that, learning to turn away from the dark, waiting always for the light to appear. While he and his former partner were still together, he went to therapy, alone because she wouldn't go, didn't see the need, saw it as his problem not hers. He read widely and tried to fix it, until he realised without her buy-in, he couldn't. So here we were, both frustrated fixers, both practised accommodators, both wary and relationship-shy.

I guide the conversation back to more brightly lit paths. I ask him about Lamarck and with the enthusiasm of a kid he expounds his love of science, his need for facts, his curiosity to know the how and why of everything. He asks about me. We clock a mutual love of cooking and admiration for Paul Keating, but sadly for me a disconnect on films and books—he doesn't read fiction, and steers clear of all those 'worthy' films with dramatic but depressing themes. Still, I am schoolgirl smitten.

Two and a half hours later at my car, we kiss. Those platform sandals again, along with the wine, the talk and the swoon I'm in, make me unsteady, and I literally topple off one, hurting my ankle. I cover up the pain and my clumsiness by laughing it off. He tells me he lives nearby and asks me to come home with him. I want to say yes. I desperately want to say yes, but with a restraint that is unusual for me, uncharacteristically wanting to keep something in reserve, I get in my car and drive away. Cool as can be, I wave and proceed to mount the median strip which I did not even see.

Next morning, I wake up to a text:

> Thanks for sleepless night.
> Me: Ditto

With my insides still churning, and my phone in hand as proof that it wasn't just me, I begin to wonder, could romantic chemistry be real? I've never given the concept much credence.

But how do you explain what happened last night? Edwin is not the sort of alpha male I'm normally attracted to. Our conversation was fascinating, but it wasn't always free-flowing. There were gaps and silences, not long enough to be awkward, but enough to suggest that Edwin is not slick in company the way Rex was. He is a beat off, but somehow, I found that endearing. I've lived with glittery confidence and this feels more honest. My morning-after attraction to Edwin feels like the real deal, the triple threat. I know it is physical, my body told me so last night, I suspect it is also emotional, though that will take some further investigation to confirm. Could it actually be chemical too? I turn to the omniscient Google: some scientists believe so called 'romantic chemistry' is the result of chemicals in your brain determining compatibility. Well, at this point, mark me down as a believer.

It's Moomba weekend and Melbourne is awash with people 'getting together and having fun'. I'd never been to a single Moomba event in my life but later in the morning when Edwin texts me to say he is taking his camera along to the parade and asks would I like to join him, I am suddenly an eager devotee—even I can put up with a bit of Moomba dagginess if it means getting to know Edwin a little better.

We agree to meet outside the Arts Centre, at the moat. I spot him first in the distance—his hat gives him away—and as I covertly walk towards him, hiding myself in the crowd, I contemplate whether to greet him with a kiss, a handshake or a simple 'Hi'. Instead I go with a tap on the shoulder and as he turns around, I sense immediately that the kiss is out. In fact, the whole connection that we'd forged the night before feels a little bit off. Edwin is guarded. The fact that it's broad daylight perhaps, or the absence of alcohol. But it's more than that. A hesitation creeps in to our conversation and a coolness takes hold. We walk side by side, looking ahead, discussing where to position ourselves for the best view, agreeing to wander, talking about anything other than what happened last night.

The parade itself is diverting enough to entertain us for an hour or two. Edwin has a proper camera and he takes lots of pictures of Viking Girls, Friendly Aliens, Polish Polka Troupes and Indigenous Warriors. He looks so adorable as he points and focuses and scans for his next subject, but I am far more focused on him and why we are stumbling than I am on the marchers. At 2 pm we are ready to rest and refuel, and it's over lunch at Pellegrini's that the reason for Edwin's reticence becomes clearer. He says he wants to take things slowly, he's not ready for what he's feeling. He needs some time. He needs to set some boundaries.

I'm not sure what those boundaries might be, but I feel so punctured, I can't even ask. I try to take heart from the fact that he is feeling something, but my damaged self says forget it, this is his goodbye speech. I feel myself shrink down to nothing, acknowledge the familiar wrench of being abandoned. I don't say anything much in return. I can't. Instead I mutely agree to whatever it is he is suggesting. On the footpath outside Pellegrini's our hug and kiss are in such contrast to last night that I feel tears prick my eyes. All the promise of that first meeting gone in a puff of smoke. As I walk home, I'm convinced I've been blown off by Edwin and that's the last I'll see of him. No doubt, the experiment will record him as 'the one that got away'.

Back home, alone on the orange two-seater, I stretch out my legs to fill the conspicuous gap. Armed with a large glass of wine and little in the way of enthusiasm, I reach for my phone and back to my buddies I go. Hello Tinder. Hello Bumble. But today there are no colourful fish in the sea.

A few days later I receive a message—it's a picture of myself copied from my work website with the caption: 'Lovely pic…sorry, but sometimes curiosity crashes through those pesky boundaries.'

So, while I'd been licking my wounds and wondering how to move on, he'd been stalking me. Of course, I'm not disappointed by this, but I am newly wary.

> Been doing your homework I see. Well at least now you know my story is legit.

> Good story—how would you like to visit my studio after I finish work on Saturday? See if I'm legit too.

I agonise over how to respond. I could go with sarcasm—isn't it a bit soon? Or play it cool—sorry I'm busy Saturday, or protect myself completely and just not answer at all, but who am I kidding? Of course, I want to see Edwin again, so instead I play it straight:

> I'd like that.

> Great, you'll find me on the corner of Little Collins and Elizabeth Street. I'm on the second floor, but if you arrive after 2 pm the door may be closed. Call me and I'll come downstairs and let you in.

Until now, all our communication had been on Tinder, via the app, so I decide to stretch the friendship.

> Okay. But how do I call you, I don't have your number.

> Boundarie (sic) warning…

Then he texts me his phone number.

I'm still not clear about the outline of the boundaries, and this time I will ask, but for now sharing a mobile number feels like progress.

How long had it been since I last smoked a bong?

It would have been in 1980 with my overland travel buddy Genevieve, in one of those pie shops in Kathmandu, so thirty-eight years ago. I only mention this now because of what happens next with Edwin.

I arrive at the designated address on the busy city corner and call Edwin from downstairs as arranged. Moments later he appears in the stairwell to unlock the door and I immediately clock the opposing jolts of attraction and panic, fighting the urge to flee. The sight of him—long and lithe, with glasses pushed up on his head, pins poked haphazardly into his shirt pocket and a tape measure draped around his neck—sends my anticipation into overload, then the memory of my recent disappointment spoils the party and reminds me how vulnerable I still am. While this internal storm between uncertainty and fear and hope and possibility rages, I follow him wordlessly up two flights of ancient stairs, along a musty corridor, past walls peeling with yellow paint, past mysterious locked doors, and finally through the last door, which chimes gaily as we enter.

Into his world. The world of a bona-fide tailor, and I'm immediately entranced by its theatricality. In a single scope of the room this is what I take in: a series of mannequins, two in full Elizabethan costume, another wearing an exact replica of Major Tom's jacket, yet another in a bridal gown immodestly waiting for a bodice. Along the wall, shoes lined up, ready to assist in the measuring of hems and heights, a massive gilt-framed mirror and two spacious changerooms with lavender satin draping. Then I look up, high above to a Victorian ceiling painted sky blue with little white clouds (just like the ones Dustin Hoffman's character painted in *Kramer vs. Kramer*). At the back of the room is a fireplace, with a fake log fire, which I'm told works in winter. The original black marble surround and mantel are still intact and at its centre is a massive oriental vase of faded plastic roses. I'm no fan of fake flowers, but somehow these ones in this room look just right.

To remind myself where I am, I wander over to the window and look down on a typical Melbourne laneway: bluestone, a street sweeper, seagulls scavenging in overflowing bins. The contrast couldn't be starker. This room has not been 'decorated'—it looks to have accumulated its charm over many years of loving occupation. While the man responsible is chatting away, presumably I'm making intelligible responses, but in truth my mind is just a little bit blown by this workplace. I'm not sure what I was expecting, but the creativity and personality on show here has definitely upped the stakes on the outcome of this day for me.

The workroom tells a different but equally revealing story. Here, I'm met by industrial-strength sewing machines and overlockers, a large cutting table, two huge cardboard bins containing rolls of fabric and drafting paper, a whole wall of cottons in every colour imaginable. The floor is littered with pins and thread, benches are strewn with fabric offcuts, scissors, unpickers, glasses (the drinking kind and the seeing kind), jackets missing arms, the remnants of a sandwich, a computer from the dark ages and a radio tuned to 774. Boxes labelled 'lace', 'facings', 'patterns', 'ribbing' perilously climb towards the ceiling. Edwin is clearly industrious but not remotely tidy.

At the end of the tour—which takes all of five minutes—we agree on the customary social diversions of a cup of tea and cake. Then, apropos of nothing, he introduces the idea of 'a little pipe'. I try to react like this is a suggestion I hear every second day, not once every thirty-eight years, so in the spirit of the experiment—and to settle my escalating nerves—I say, 'Sure, why not?' hoping like hell I don't make a massive fool of myself and that I remember how to inhale and don't choke on the smoke.

While Edwin boils the kettle, sets out the cups and packs a pipe made from a Dare iced-coffee container (good to see he's giving those single-use plastics a second life), I sit on the kidney-shaped client sofa and try to place Edwin in these rooms, fitting frocks to women's bodies, shortening cuffs on stout men, cutting patterns from pictures ripped from magazines, managing egos and gently reframing expectations. I imagine him, part craftsman, part conjuror, part counsellor and wonder how just being good at one thing, like sewing, can equip someone with the skills required to wear so many different hats. Interrupting my ruminations, and handing me a slice of carrot cake on a chipped floral plate, is the man-enigma I hope to decode a little further today.

Turns out my bong skills are indeed rusty, but after a mildly embarrassing coughing fit, quelled by tea and Edwin's good humour, I'm emboldened enough to suggest we take a walk. 'It's a beautiful today and we could head towards my place through the Botanical Gardens.'

Edwin agrees readily, and as we shuffle through the autumn leaves we switch between talking and walking in a comfortable silence. I don't remember much of what we said. What I do remember is feeling a lightness (not just a light-headedness) and a youthfulness that was as much a surprise to me as the fact that I'm stoned for the first time in nearly four decades.

It's after four by the time we arrive. I open a bottle of

pinot gris and we settle in on the orange two-seater. I learn about his family. He has a son, now twenty-six, but has never married. He and his son and his son's mum made things work and are still on good terms. His own mum and dad are still alive, he has one older brother and one younger sister—so he's a middle child. His sewing, which started out of need, fashioning the clothes and costumes he and his friends wanted to wear to nightclubs in the eighties, but couldn't find (or afford) in shops had developed into a successful business. So, a self-taught craftsman whose hobby had stuck and whose other skills, the people-pleasing ones I was speculating about earlier had, according to Edwin, not come naturally, but developed over time and out of necessity. Edwin is not easy to pigeonhole and he is nothing like Rex, both of which make him intriguing to me. Even his deep interest in science, which seems so at odds with his craft, is hard to work out. But then he tells me that it's the problem-solving part of his job that he loves best, that science comes into everything, even working out the exact way a bias cut can flatter a fulsome hip. I frown at that and he says, 'Without a pattern you have to run your own experiments and persist until you get it right.'

Our conversation doesn't once feel gratuitous or forced, or confined by self-imposed 'boundaries'. I bring up the 'dreaded boundaries' of our previous date. He explains that after the demise of his last relationship, which he thought would be for life, he is freshly wary. He's baffled by his propensity to make it to the medium term with his partners, but never beyond. His conclusion—it's easy to fall in love, much harder to stay in love. This time, at this age, he wants someone to stick, to grow old with, so he's determined to take more time over his choice. I get it, respect it even, but I know that it will be a test for me, because I'm impetuous and needy and greedy for this man. Of course, if I can go with it, his strategy would surely be good for me too, but while I'm sitting here at peak arousal, I'm wondering just how slow is slow?

To change the topic, I ask if he's getting hungry. 'Yes,' he says, as he reaches towards me, 'I am. But let's just try this first.'

This is not 'safe' like it was with Rudy. Edwin has just laid his cards on the table and there's danger at every turn in the path we are about to go down. Intimacy can make a mockery of the best laid plans and ruthlessly cast common sense aside, but by the same token it will rarely be denied. When his hands cradle my face and our lips meet, memories flood back to me about how good it feels to be kissed by someone you really like. Especially someone you don't yet know, but would like to know a whole lot better. It's completely different to kissing with the established comfort of familiarity. It's loaded with the desire you've hoarded during the long winter of abstinence, charged with hungry hormones.

Two hours later, we really are ravenous, and as we

come back downstairs, we survey the carnage left by libido unleashed. Little pools of clothes on the floor, underwear tangled with jeans, a watch between the couch cushions, an upturned wine glass. It's like a scene from a movie, the kind you never think happens in real life.

Edwin has put on an old sarong of mine and I am in my green cotton robe. I open the fridge which has definitely not been prepared for this eventuality. I find some flatbread, some broccolini, some goats cheese, a jar of anchovies and some barely presentable basil. As I pull together makeshift pizzas, Edwin takes charge of the music and his playlist is pitch perfect: Bryan Ferry, Portishead, the Cure, Grace Jones, Dire Straits. We return to what's left of the pinot gris and take our pizzas outside.

It's a beautiful autumn night—sultry and still, and the light reflected from the low cloud cover bathes my little courtyard in a glow that mirrors how I feel.

When Frankie Goes to Hollywood's 'Relax' comes on, Edwin gets up and does a little impromptu dance. A sexy, semi-naked man is dancing in my backyard. Is this really happening to me? At this age, at this stage of my life?

After 'Perfect Day' by Lou Reed, we decide to call it a night and go to bed.

Together.

Sleeping together—that is, trying to achieve restful unconsciousness with a stranger—is nothing like 'sleeping together'.

It's really tricky. You haven't yet established your patterns. The initial skin contact (happening for real now, not on a wine list) is deliriously good, but it's not long before you get all hot and sweaty and have to move. Problem is, you don't know the person well enough to know if this will cause offence. Is he ready to untangle yet? Will I disturb him? Can I hang in here a bit longer? No, I really need to move.

Then there are sides of the bed and sleeping positions to be negotiated. You listen for the rhythmic breath of sleep and it doesn't come. After a couple of restless hours, he suggests he might move next door to the spare bed where at least he can 'fart with freedom'. Romance killer? Perhaps, but in my view that kind of candour is a definite relationship builder.

On Monday morning, I walk to work feeling liberated, loved-up, invincible. And the cosmos seems to sense it. People nod, flirt, make eye contact and smile as if they see my secret. The vibe I am putting out is the vibe I am getting back. I am wide open, transmitting and receiving.

But now what? The inevitable doubt creeps in. The head starts to pose all those pesky questions that I thought I'd finished with in adolescence. Who makes the next move? How is he feeling? What is the accepted time interval between contact?

Can't appear too keen. Don't want to be too cool.

Do I thank him for a lovely time—never been my style—or do I just sit tight and wait?

Let me tell you, none of this gets any easier with age. Above all, I don't want to blow it. But my radar for what's right is decidedly rusty. In fact, I suspect many of my friends might say I was never a good judge.

Monday passes, Tuesday morning passes and my bubble is in severe need of air. I'm working alongside Eliza in our new office. Trying to concentrate, trying to adjust to the fact that we have traded our business independence for a more secure future, employment longevity for her, and an exit strategy for me. We'd recently finalised a deal to merge with a larger company, which meant we were no longer bosses, but employees once again. At about 4 pm, I get a message from our new receptionist saying that the neighbours at our vacated former office in Willis Street have called to say that there's a bunch of flowers on the doorstep, which have been there since yesterday. They have my name on them.

I run the 500 metres back to our old building (still listed as our current business address on our website), all the way willing them to be from Edwin, but cautioning myself that they'll more likely be from Rudy or Dean or my solicitor who's making a fortune out of my separation. When I get there, I retrieve a beautiful bunch of simple pink lilies. I open the envelope and the card reads, 'Fuck Your Anxiety'.

No signature, nothing else, but I am somersault happy.

Let me explain: at some point during our late-night picnic in my courtyard, Edwin was trying to warn me that he can sometimes be quite an anxious person. Something triggered by an early childhood incident that therapists have cautioned will always be with him and surface from time to time, especially when he feels pressured or gets sick. Normally an empathetic and understanding listener, I cut him off and said dismissively, 'Fuck your anxiety, Edwin.'

I can't believe I said that, that I could be so callous, and in the face of him revealing something so intensely personal. Of course, what I really meant was, let's not spoil this moment by getting too deep, too soon. That mixed with memories of Rex's mental issues still fresh in my mind. To Edwin's great credit, he heard me and moved on. But having the wit to throw it back at me on his first greeting card? That showed real class. Not to mention an adorable sense of self-deprecation.

While this burgeoning love story is taking place in the foreground, there is an almighty war being waged in the background. What looked like a simple and amicable agreement between Rex and me to split our assets fifty–fifty has devolved into an acrimonious fight between his solicitor (hereinafter known as the Rottweiler) and mine.

It all went off the rails when I suggested to Rex—quite practically I thought—that we might put the house on the market, allowing us to split the proceeds. Clean, easy, no fuss, and house prices were looking pretty good.

But Rex didn't want to move. Nor did he want to pay top dollar to buy me out. He was dug in, boots and all, not only to the house (where he was now blissfully ensconced with Anna) but also to the notion, latterly suggested by the Rottweiler, that he was entitled to half of my business, the value of which was virtually unquantifiable since the merger that had us working as employees for the next three years on an earnout basis.

It took twelve months, during which time we amassed files too large to carry and wasted untold sums of money in fees, before the Rottweiler could be convinced that there was no pot of gold at the end of the Working Girls rainbow. That didn't stop him sniffing under every log and pissing on every proposal we put forward, before finally offering us a 'generous' sixty–forty settlement of all assets, including the house and the business. In Rex's favour.

Seeing that in writing, I saw scarlet, vermilion, crimson, carmine, magenta, blood and every other shade of red you care to name. I literally punched a wall, and while I hopped around the lounge room shaking my scraped knuckles to quell the pain, I ran the facts: Rex had cheated on me, I was the injured party, I was the one who'd had to go and find a place to rent, I was the one whose life had been totally dislocated, I was the one who'd had to set up from scratch, I was the one in therapy, I was the one still working, I was the one who had contributed the lion's share to our 'joint assets'.

And yet it seemed *I* was going to have to pay *him* for the privilege of him shitting all over me.

When my scraped knuckles finally stopped throbbing, I phoned my solicitor—a glorious calm woman—and said, 'Call the cunts and tell them we're going to court!'

That worked. They backed off quicker than Wile E. Coyote pursued by the Road Runner, but still I came off second best. The final split was fifty-two–forty-eight in Rex's favour, based on the fact that he was older than me and therefore had less earning potential.

He had retired for fuck's sake—voluntarily!

The hot glow of summer is gone, now it's the melancholy light of autumn that weakly warms my face as I lie on the orange couch, the change of seasons reminding me that the time elapsed since the split is growing. Ten months now. So much has changed, Eliza was right about time, you just have to do it and see where it takes you. Today I grapple with a new problem, one that is hardly a problem at all in the recent sense of the word, but still, I have to do something about it. Rudy and I are still exchanging texts full of newsy updates and plans for our reunion. His description of the mountains, differently beautiful without the glamour of snow, and his hard labour on the steep hillsides suggest a brutal physicality I want to share. I always imagined him back in my bed, his pictures and texts fuelling the fantasy. But now of course I have a dilemma. Edwin. Selfishly I don't want to give up my contract with Rudy for unencumbered mutual pleasure. After only one encounter, it feels like unfinished business. More than that it's a clear horizon to a mystery place that marriage never allowed.

But it feels dishonest to be making plans with Rudy, when I am feeling very attracted to someone else. I liken my luck on Tinder to falling pregnant after the very first round of IVF. Since becoming an unlikely evangelist for the dating apps, I have sung their praises to anyone who will listen, many younger than me, only to hear that they have had widely varying experiences, some positive, others swearing off them forever because their encounters have been either frustrating, demeaning or downright scary. But here am I, after six dates facing what feels like a real choice. A no-strings lover? Or, potentially, a many-stringed mate for life?

I rely on Rudy's EI when I tell him what's going on and I am gratified by his response. I explain that I was really looking forward to seeing him again, but that from somewhere way beyond the beam of my radar I have been plucked to explore something I never thought possible. The chance to make a real connection later in life. And even though I am reluctant to jump into another serious relationship so soon, the idea of exploring one last shot at 'love' seems like an opportunity too good to let slip.

From Rudy:
> Jo, you are being blessed by the universe.
> More than happy for you...from my heart,
> go, enjoy, explore and whoopee if it continues
> to develop. Get back to me if it all goes pear
> shaped.

Remember dating? That delirious whirl of testing, second-guessing, anticipation, projection, excitement and self-doubt? Well, try doing it at sixty when you're completely out of practice.

I was pretty keen to impress Edwin with my social range and 'try anything' approach but, in truth, my recent experience of any outing that would qualify as entertainment, beyond a restaurant or movie or a monthly book club meeting, was pretty slim. Then, one evening when I was driving to yoga in St Kilda, I saw it. The Palais—that endearingly derelict and romantic building next to Luna Park—was showing upcoming concert dates for Sérgio Mendes & Brasil '66. I don't profess to being a jazz/samba aficionado, nor do I know anything about said band other than that my cool cousins used to play their records at the beach house back in the 60s, but I fixed on the idea that this would be a sure-fire winner for my first date with Edwin. We'd agreed to go out on Friday night and I had promised to surprise him.

As soon as I got home from yoga I hopped online and booked tickets, feeling pretty chuffed, because who doesn't love the Palais, and surely some lively Latin vibes would make me look worldly and musically hip. Even the early start was working for me, because Edwin doesn't know it yet, but I tend to flag pretty soon after 9.30. It's not an age thing, just something I've lived with and been mocked for all my life. How was I to know that most of the concert would be taken up by Sergio's wife centre-stage singing Gold FM standards in a series of bad ballgowns, while Sergio and the ageing 66ers faithfully kept time in the background? No 'Spanish Flea', no 'Going out of my Head'. None of their famous back catalogue. Even the promoters tried to sauce things up a bit with a guest appearance midway through by some young rapper, but that just seemed misplaced and weird. I sat through the whole concert, conscious that Edwin was trying his best to send some positivity my way with occasional foot-tapping, but realising that this choice was not going to give me the big credibility boost I was after.

For our next date it was his turn to choose and he continued with the musical theme, booking tickets to see Max Reibl, a counter tenor, at the Butterfly Club, located down a discreet laneway in the city. I didn't even know what a counter tenor was at the time, but he did, having seen Max previously, and he knew what a treat I was in for. Especially at the Butterfly Club, a tiny venue that put us only metres away from Max and his pianist, close enough to see the sweat on his forehead and catch his spittle in the footlights. He opened the show with an extraordinary rendition of 'Skyfall', then toured us back in time, to more traditional counter-tenor territory with a series of soul-shattering Baroque arias. I'd had no idea what to expect, but I hadn't imagined anything like this. I was literally moved to tears by the miracle of his voice, by the very idea that human vocal chords, indeed one man's vocal chords, could be coaxed into such wildly disparate places and with such force. But the biggest surprise was yet to come. For his finale, Max fast-forwarded five centuries and delivered a version of Nirvana's 'Smells Like Teen Spirit' that I'm sure would have had Kurt Cobain cheering from the grave. The show ended with Max and his pianist taking their final bows and leaving the stage, while we just sat, rooted to our seats, me trying to find the words to wrap around what I was feeling. Transcendent joy for the intimacy of the experience. Disbelief and gratitude that I was here. Piqued that Edwin had so comprehensively outdone me. I gave up on the words, instead I found Edwin's hand, wiped more tears from my cheeks and said, 'I need a drink.'

Admittedly Max Reibl was always going to be a hard act to follow, but our subsequent date, also Edwin's choice, an indoor rock-climbing venue where we were mainly surrounded by kids having birthday parties with their sugar-fuelled friends, turned out to be more laughable than laudable. In the safety briefing, I'm sure we were the only people over five foot, and we did feel kind of stupid having to chorus the call of 'Look Out Below' along with fifty excited pint-sized climbers.

Determining where to go for dates was stressful enough, but by far my biggest bouts of anxiety were reserved for the act of deciding what I would wear when we were going out. Edwin's business is clothes and he has a very particular and attractive (to me) sense of style. I asked him to describe it one time and he eventually came up with 'deconstructed dandy'. Regardless of the label, he always managed to look just right, be it rock-climbing, going out or simply cooking in my kitchen.

Against all my expectations Tinder had served me up a man who could rock a cravat and a hat without looking the slightest bit affected. Even his tracky daks were cool: faded red old-style adidas, not too tight, not too loose. And here was I, suddenly conscious that my predilection for mannish, black and oversized, which I had always found comfortable and stylish in a subversive sort of way, was revealed for what it was: lazy and boring.

I joked to my friends that while most people found getting naked in front of a new lover intimidating, I was the opposite. I felt fine in the nude, but choosing what to wear just about brought on a panic that resulted in that familiar female trope of clothes strewn from one end of the bedroom to the other.

Not that Edwin was critical. He just started making me things and bringing home vintage shop finds that in a former life I would not have looked twice at. He was a much better shopper for me than I was for myself. Bit by bit, my wardrobe changed. He added colour, print, shape and self-esteem to my repertoire. Dresses even, which I had long since stopped wearing. When Edwin asked me why, I couldn't really say, except that I felt dresses were for girls and somehow, I didn't qualify. Nonsense he said, you look great in dresses.

My metamorphosis started to show and people at work started to notice. They complimented me on my appearance. Not just my clothes, but the happiness that now radiated from my whole being. Still, the man responsible remained a mystery to them, and to all of my friends, because I was not ready yet to make him public.

Our agreement to take things slowly settled into a pattern that seemed to work for us both. Edwin lived on the other side of town and didn't drive a car. He used a bike for transport, and carried most of his life around in two panniers and a backpack. On Friday nights, after work, he would ride 'Condor', his lovingly resurrected roadside find to my place, stay the weekend, then return to work on Monday and spend weeknights with his housemates in Brunswick. It worked for Edwin because it gave him time to put distance between me and his previous partner and it worked for me because I'd become pretty protective of my new-found independence and needed those four nights to myself.

Then, one Saturday morning about a month into this arrangement, there came a moment of truth that I had completely wiped from my mind. We were lying in bed and Edwin asked, 'When's your birthday?'

Without thinking I replied, 'April 17th.'

'Oh, that's soon, so you'll be what fifty-eight, fifty-nine?'

I had completely forgotten about the Tinder trap.

He sees my response and ventures. 'Oh, is it the big one?'

'Actually,' I say, swallowing a huge lump of dread, 'I've already had the big one. It's the one after that.'

He goes quiet. Then he goes to the bathroom. For a very long time.

Edwin is fifty-four and in a few weeks time I'll be sixty-one. Seven years looks like a lot on a birth certificate, but it doesn't feel that way when we're together. I reckon most people would pick us as being similar in age, and there's even a small spike of pride that I am reversing a societal trend that would almost always go the other way. But suddenly, as I wait for Edwin to return, I feel vulnerable, relegated once again to redundant older woman, not to mention being caught out in a lie.

Silently he climbs back into bed beside me, and I say, 'That's a deal-breaker then, is it?' feeling for sure that it will be.

He's lying on his back, looking at the ceiling, when he

says, 'No, not necessarily. But you've just given me some new information that I'll have to process—that we'll have to process. It's not the age difference that matters to me Jo. The problem is that we're at different life stages. You're probably ready to wind back at work, travel, take off. But I still have a lot of hard slog ahead of me, a business I can't leave, no real assets. I don't want to hold you back, but I'm not in a position to join you either.'

I remember his wish to grow old with someone, but concede he probably wasn't reckoning on me having such a head start.

My heart sinks, because what he says is true. Separately, silently, we process the implications of the revelation. Finding each other so quickly was something neither of us envisaged. Now there's a new consideration in the mix. And it's not even the telling of the porky on Tinder that bites, it's the reality. Reality bites.

For the rest of the weekend, we move warily around each other and the giant elephant in the room. The apartment suddenly feels cramped rather than cosy, the silence an awkward reminder of our premature and probably foolhardy future projection. Edwin leaves early on Sunday afternoon with nothing really resolved except the commitment to think about it. And from the moment he closes the door I do little else myself.

The thing about being dumped by someone you thought you loved (and who you thought loved you) is that you no longer trust your feelings or your judgment. Having spent the past thirty years of my life living with one person, despite how deficient or disappointing that person might have been at times, I was still finding it incredibly hard to make way for a new one. For the best part of my marriage to Rex, I held firm to the conviction that he and I were good together simply because we had similar tastes and common interests. We read the same books, agreed on movies. We ran a house together, ate together, rode together, walked together, golfed together. We still sunbaked (as wrong as that was) and swam at the beach. Our travel plans were always easy because we wanted to go to the same places. We loved dogs and dim sims and Leonard Cohen and a million other little things. Our commonality was the glue that held us together.

Until it didn't.

Now I was trying to determine where Edwin fitted in my life. In some absurd way, I was missing the drama and excitement that was part of life with Rex. He was very good at being charming, keeping things interesting and keeping me constantly on my toes, which leaves the average nice guy at a distinct disadvantage. Not that I thought Edwin was average in any way. But he was indisputably nice, and I found myself measuring him against a flawed ideal that I stubbornly refused to let go. With Rex I was used to fireworks, the passionate kind and the destructive kind. I'd learned to function in the face of both, and I'd become the high priestess of the highwire act. I was not familiar with constancy, an even temperament, consideration or tenderness. If I'm to be really honest, it felt a bit boring.

No sooner do I frame that thought than it stings me with a slap of shame. After all this time and all that work, am I really still that person? It becomes clear during this thinking time that instead of looking for an improved version of Rex, I needed to admit change in myself and embrace difference in my partner. It would be the next big challenge of the experiment and, depending on where Edwin landed after our four days apart, I hoped I'd have the chance to work with him on what a new relationship might look like.

To begin, I revert to a fail-safe strategy and draw up a list.

THE LEDGER OF LIKES

EDWIN	JO
Facts	Fiction
Science fiction	Real-life drama
War, history	Popular culture, art
Anything old	Anything modern
Snow, cold	Beach, warm
Noodling	Planning
Hoarding	Decluttering
Ambling	Striding
Flea markets	Boutiques
Radio National	Triple J
Classical music	Classic rock
Fried food	Seafood

Anything in crumbs	Anything fresh
Fitted	Loose
Being home	Being away
Weed	Wine
Blinds closed	Blinds always open

Clearly, if Edwin and I were ever going to make it, 'twinning' was not going to be the glue that kept us together. Yet I didn't see this list with its counterpoints as a problem. Instead, I treated it as a challenge. There was nothing in there that I'd call a deal-breaker (except if he couldn't get used to sleeping with the blinds open) and, importantly, we had already established accord on the big three:

Sex (yes), Politics (left) and Religion (no).

It got to Thursday before I heard from Edwin, but that night I received a simple text asking if it was okay for him to come over after work tomorrow as usual. So, I replied in kind: Yes. Not knowing if he was coming to let me down in person and leave, or stay the weekend.

On Friday I chilled some wine, set out some almonds and olives and started to listen for the sound of his bike pulling up outside my door. Just after six, I let him in and stood like stone in the middle of the room while he stuffed his backpack under the stairs, helped himself to a glass of water, and removed his shoes.

Then he came to me, arms lifted, a waft of his signature

sweat on the air, before he encircled me and said, 'I can't let you slip through my fingers.'

That was it, possibly the most beautiful thing I'd ever heard. Someone wanted to hold on to me.

Later, I showed him my list and he agreed we could work on that but for now we had some reconnecting to do.

Next morning in bed the issue of my birthday was raised again. 'What would you like to do?' Edwin asked.

'Apart from pretend it's not happening, you mean?'

'Yes, apart from that, which I am perfectly okay with, just so you know.'

'Well, for about the past thirty years I have spent it with Eve and Martin—and Rex. Are you ready to be my Rex replacement?'

'Well, that depends—are you?'

This was big for me. So far, I'd kept Edwin and my friends separate. Keeping him a secret kept him safe. Us safe. I'd avoided introducing him to anyone in order to delay the inevitable judgment that would follow. Only when things fell apart did any of my friends dare tell me what they really thought of Rex. What would happen now? Would they be doubly protective of me and therefore doubly hard on Edwin. Or would they flip the other way and say they liked him even if they didn't. How could I trust them to tell me the truth and, more importantly, could I handle the truth? Why was this such a big deal? That's one question I could answer. Because my friends have been my lifeblood pretty much my whole life, substituting for family and being there for me through the very worst. I owe them—lots of them old friends whose opinion, rightly or wrongly, mattered to me.

When my world first exploded and I moved in with Eve and Martin, they jokingly referred to me as 'the kid'. I, in turn, called them Mum and Dad. So, it stood to reason that the first people to meet Edwin should be them. We decided on a low-key birthday celebration at my place where Edwin and I would cook together, break bread and break the ice with Eve and Martin as two couples.

On the day, I woke to a mild feeling of panic, the kind you might expect if you were due to deliver a big speech. I could feel myself progressively going off the rails as the day went on. I overcomplicated the menu and made dishes that required way too much last-minute attention. I cleaned like Eve and Martin were not friends, but health inspectors. I worried about what to wear and made Edwin change three times before I was happy with his outfit. I set the table and reset the table. The table for four that would feature Edwin in Rex's place.

Then as soon as the doorbell rang it triggered a level of anxiety in me that I could neither contain nor explain. I was terror-stricken and incompetent all at once. Eve and Martin gave me some yoga-related birthday presents which I opened and promptly put aside. I went to get them drinks but forgot what they wanted. I couldn't sit still, but my constant flurry failed to achieve anything constructive. I'd go out to the courtyard to check the barbeque, see the fish cakes were falling apart and come back to the oven because that felt all too hard to deal with. I'd look at the giant snapper wrapped in foil, as if by looking I was doing something, but then I'd close the oven door without so much as a finger prod of the fish. And in the background people kept talking! What were they saying? I had no idea. Was I being asked a question, it seemed so, as everyone was looking at me expectantly. Edwin who, thank goodness, really can cook, clocked the mayhem in my mind, diplomatically leaving his new friends at the table to bring the meal home, while his crazy new girlfriend swung between babbled nonsense and catatonic silence.

In my mind the stakes were simply too high. I kept comparing the easy camaraderie of our old four-way friendship with the high tension of this situation. Tension that was, of course, all of my making, all in my mind, but also beyond my power to control. As soon as Eve and Martin left, I collapsed on Edwin's shoulder, aware I'd made a complete mess of the evening.

Later that night, as we lie in bed, I try to explain the reason for my bizarre behaviour. But it wasn't easy, because I didn't really understand it myself. Except to say that in the moment, the picture felt all wrong. There was a strange man in the place Rex had occupied for thirty years by my side, alongside Eve and Martin. And the actualisation of that threw me completely off kilter.

I come back to my judgment, the thing I can no longer locate let alone trust, and I find myself wondering again if Edwin is right for me.

Eve and Martin text to say they'd had a lovely evening and they think Edwin is great. (I wonder, were they at the same party as me?) Edwin says he liked them too but thought Martin was a bit hard on me. Yes, he was, but how do I begin to explain to Edwin that the mocking sense of humour on display tonight has been part of our friendship for ever. We're hard on each other, that's how we roll, with Rex the undisputed king of the cutting comment. I wonder where that leaves me now. Edwin's compassion and consideration feel so foreign. After years of building up a resilience that I felt proud of, it feels a bit weak to allow tenderness. To be needy. Surely, I didn't need that. I am tough, I am strong, I am self-sufficient.

Actually, who was I kidding? I am a bloody mess.

Long into the night, we keep talking, revealing, feeling our way along the pitted paths of total disclosure. I admit to Edwin that I am having trouble trusting my feelings, especially as those feelings keep switching allegiances. Most times I want nothing more than to be rid of Rex for good, then I miss his jokes and our puppies, even his stupid put-downs. How is that possible? I tell Edwin of the relief I'd felt when he said he wanted to hang on to me, but following hot on the heels of that came the catastrophising.

I worried he might hurt me, or take advantage of me or that I'd allow myself to be compromised all over again. I say that sometimes the most powerful attraction of all is the pull of my new and surprisingly enjoyable independence. Then I remember I'm sixty and I'd be facing a long walk alone if I don't have someone to share the rest of my life with. Perhaps it all boils down to this: I want someone, but I am terrified of getting it wrong again.

Finally, Edwin shoots down every objection with this one exhausted thought. 'Jo what have we got to lose? For some reason Zeus has thrown us together and it's not like I'm auditioning to be the father of your children.'

Through deep fatigue I manage a laugh and concede he is right. At my age why would I be wasting time wondering if this is my forever man, when forever is an ever-decreasing abstraction that could end any day? There are other things like living arrangements and age differences and list anomalies to be negotiated, but without the burden of these weighty considerations, the pressure valve is released enormously, and it feels okay to finally say: 'Yeah, let's just give it a go.'

Easter arrives soon after the night of the big birthday reckoning, which gives Edwin and me the chance to spend some quality time together away from work. Four days in the constant company of each other to test our compatibility and our differences and start giving it a 'red hot go'.

On Good Friday, we take a long leisurely bike ride along the Yarra to Dights Falls, which I had never visited before. I'm pleasantly surprised that with Edwin cycling is not a race and as we roll along side by side, we talk about who actually lives in those huge river-facing mansions, and why do you never see anyone in them, how much it would take for Edwin to strip down to his undies and swim across the Yarra ($500)—too cheap, I say—when Edwin will come over to the dark side and wear lycra (never), who is the Dight of Dights Falls (will need to google that). On the way home we discuss what we'll make for dinner, settling on a spinach and cheese pie which will keep God happy because it contains no meat, and me too—Rex was never that keen on vego.

That night, we decided to watch a movie, which occasions our first big session at the negotiation table. I suggest *Call Me by Your Name*. He reads the synopsis and says, 'Too worthy.' He suggests *Avatar*, and I flat out refuse because it contains fake blue people. So we compromise on *The Shape of Water*, which disappoints us both equally. In the world of compromise is that a win?

That night, I set the alarm for 7.30, and he asks, 'Why?'

'Because I'm going to yoga.'

'Really. But—'

'But—what? I always go to yoga on Saturday morning.'

'But I have the day off and I usually have to work

on Saturday, so couldn't you make an exception just for tomorrow?'

Another compromise and it's only day two.

I realise then that charting a successful course through any new relationship, but especially a late-in-life one, is going to be a real challenge. The key will be how well we can negotiate change. Or, from the other side of the coin, how fixed we have become in our ways. We'll be forced to consider what we are prepared to flex on, what we can forgive, how open we can be, and what parts of ourselves and our habits are non-negotiable. It's early days, but I hope compromise isn't going to spell the end of spontaneity and smooth the interesting edges off everything.

On Saturday, after I didn't go to yoga, I make Edwin sit on the bed while I try on every single item in my wardrobe. He had to vote—'keep', 'chuck' or 'renovate'. I end up with three piles I am very happy with. The reduced 'keep' pile makes room for breathing space between the hangers. The 'chuck' pile, two huge bags, is destined for the op shop, and the 'renovate' pile is stuff he'd take to work and return reinvented for a second life. Next day, Sunday morning, he gets up early and with my blessing goes to the Coburg market alone, as he has been doing for years. So much for decluttering—he returns around midday with a black-and-white bouclé coat, a pair of navy and black Ark jacquard leggings, a Christian Lacroix silk shirt in pastel shades of lavender and lemon, a pair of Gap checked stretch pants and a fabulous Omikron man's wristwatch with a black face and fluoro green digits. All for me, and all going straight to the keep pile.

I get to wear my new second-hand bouclé coat that night as I have bought tickets to see Kitty Flanagan at the Melbourne Comedy Festival. Edwin suggests we leave a bit earlier and make a pitstop at Christ Church on the corner of Toorak and Punt roads, whose noticeboard issues an open invitation to all to join the evening chorale service. I feel slightly uncomfortable as a non-believer going into a church at Easter, but we slide inconspicuously into a back pew and the voices are worth any retribution God may elect to dish out.

Back on the tram to the Athenaeum, Edwin takes a call from his mum. I am slightly gobsmacked and genuinely touched to hear how tender and caring he is towards her. So often the men I have known put their mums in the obligatory column and give their time begrudgingly. Maybe I've just mixed with the wrong men, but Edwin keeps surprising me with his kindness and complete lack of artifice.

And at Kitty's show I am about to be surprised again. He squirms through the whole thing, clearly uncomfortable, not enjoying the humour. Admittedly there are some jokes that cut close to the bone—about online dating and men who make loud toilet noises on first sleepovers—but I find it hilarious. Mind you, having a non-responsive partner beside you can kind of spoil the fun. Turns out stand-up comedy makes Edwin uneasy. All that mocking, taking easy shots, setting up 'in groups' and 'out groups'. I want to say yeah, but comedy comes from social observation and what's more Kitty's world view aligns pretty closely with mine, and if you don't like her, what does that say about me and us? But I don't say that, because I remember that I am meant to be embracing difference. I just chalk it up as another lesson in Relationships 101 at the University of the New Age.

By the time Easter is over I am ready for some time alone. I experience that blissful feeling of relief when house guests finally leave, everything goes quiet and you have your space back to yourself. I open the fridge and take two bites out of a cucumber, before putting it back in the crisper, then I reach for my tweezers and magnifying mirror and go out into the courtyard, where the light is good, to pluck the rogue chin hairs I can feel poking through.

Winter announces itself in Melbourne as one of the wettest and coldest on record and my urban ski-chalet flat is nowhere near as fortified as one in the mountains would be. For starters there's no heating, no insulation and the old timber window frames are so rotten they provide easy access for the cold air, and the rain too, when the wind is from the south, providing the unique experience of being rained on in bed. So I'm grateful for Edwin's company and for the extra body warmth. Together we plug gaps with Blu Tack and Spakfilla, pile blankets on the orange couch and hunker down in front of the new portable electric heater I rush out to buy one especially bitter Sunday, and continue our exploration of each other.

I discover that Edwin is a man of ritual. He has porridge for breakfast every morning made with grated pear and oatmilk and topped with strawberries (in season) and walnuts. This is followed by two pieces of toast with olive oil and Promite, then a strong coffee. Can I have a serious relationship with a man who puts oil on toast instead of butter, and prefers Promite to Vegemite? It seems very unAustralian. He works six days a week and rides his bike in any weather. He never complains. He flosses every night. Buys a scratchie every Saturday.

He is also, as I observed in his work environment, obliviously untidy. His keys, phone, Aldi catalogue, riding gloves and random pocket detritus are dumped on the nearest clear surface, usually one I have just tidied. And you'd be amazed by how much thread and fluff stick to a man who sews for a living and trails behind him wherever he goes, collecting even in his navel. This is in stark contrast to my clean-and-tidy tendencies, which are off the scale in the opposite direction, so clearly compromise will be on constant call.

Despite the challenges of the weather and long-ingrained habits, winter brings us closer. We start to prefer staying in to going out, with most of our best times spent in the kitchen cooking. On Saturday mornings we take our jeep (procured by Edwin from a dump bin and reupholstered with black vinyl) to the Prahran market and shop fresh for the weekend, creating menus on the fly, according to what looked good and what we felt like. At around 5 pm Edwin ramps up his disco, I pour the prosecco and we cook and dance around the tiny galley kitchen, and each other, with Aretha and Prince and Elvis Costello providing the soundtrack to our happiness.

It's in the kitchen where we discover our second-best compatibility. Edwin is a gun baker and pastry chef, while I'm more your umami-inclined main-course-maker. So serendipity reigns supreme, with the gold-medal meal so far, my seafood paella followed by Edwin's frangipane tart.

PART 4

Expansion

Changing my wardrobe. Broadening my music tastes. Being less demented about exercise. Sleeping in. Re-using, recycling and repurposing. All these are positive changes in my life that arrive with Edwin. That winter he opened my eyes to how much money I spent through sheer thoughtlessness. Especially when it came to those big black shapeless garments that usually had a designer label and an eye-watering price tag to match. He took me to his favourite markets and vintage shops where we'd find ten fabulous one-off pieces that would cost less than one pair of leggings at Lululemon.

He has encouraged me to be less hard on myself about keeping fit and getting fat, while I have encouraged him to be more conscious of his health, his time and his priorities. I've improved his diet with dishes that are so tasty he doesn't realise they are healthy. He bakes cakes that are so irresistible I've had to put my sugar aversion on hold. Despite my early dismissive outburst, I've helped him to recognise and manage his anxiety. On the points where we can't meet, we simply give the other their space. While I watch the likes of *My Brilliant Friend* and *Ozark*, he sits contentedly beside me on the orange sofa going down endless internet rabbit holes in search of new facts about topics as diverse as ancient Greek democracy and what makes a sponge cake so light.

My personal 'expansion' has come with an added bonus. I've let other people into my life too. Lots of new ones, like Samantha, who is now a firm friend, and Greta the counsellor/Buddhist from the yoga retreat, who fulfills my need for challenging conversation, and quite a few old ones have returned too, casualties of my former capitulation to social harmony. It comes as something of an epiphany to me now to see how far I had let my relationship with Rex narrow my life, shrink my horizons, curb my personality.

With Edwin I feel I can be a more authentic version of myself. It certainly helps to be able to go back to a blank canvas and start again. With the benefit of a new beginning, I feel able to show myself without fear of being judged or rebuked. I could announce my intention to spend a weekend away with the girls, or suggest a play at Red Stitch, without first having to carefully pick my time and then steel myself for the default response of 'No'. I can't tell you how liberating that is, how gratifying that the more *me* I am, the more Edwin seems to like me, and no matter how often I experience it, I am taken aback by the unexpected pleasure of being with someone whose default position is 'Yes'.

So, towards the end of winter, when Edwin asks me if I'd like to come away with him and some visiting English friends for a long weekend at Falls Creek, I can't very well say no, though I have lots of reasons why I want to—no, I don't like the cold; no, I'm too old to learn to ski; no, I'm nervous about going away with people I don't know; no, I don't have any ski gear; no, I don't want you to see me fail at something. Instead, I just suck it all up and say, 'Yes.'

This is our first road trip together. My first with someone other than Rex. I've borrowed a helmet and apres-ski boots from Eliza, bought a cheap ski parka and pants from Aldi, cooked Karen Martini's Syrian chicken and lentil soup, packed loads of chocolate and mandarins (essential for the slopes, Edwin tells me) wine and whisky, and I'm prepared to meet my doom.

Edwin has booked a modest chalet that will sleep us in one double room and his friends and their two teenage boys in a bunk room for four. They are arriving the day after us, so on night one we have the place to ourselves.

It's just like home, but warmer and drier. And I immediately love it. The first thing that strikes me is the silence of snow. The stillness. And—when I refuse, against Edwin's urging, to wear the snow boots—the slipperiness. We are unloading the car when I land flat on my arse, dropping a heavy box of groceries on the hard-packed snow and feeling the sting of Edwin's 'told you so'. He doesn't say it, but it's there plain to see on his face.

The next morning, we wake up to a bluebird day, and Edwin tells me I should feel blessed because not everyone gets to see one. But after I fall three times just trying to snowplough my way to the ski lift, I don't feel blessed at all—I feel clumsy and exposed, and I'm sure Edwin wishes he hadn't suggested this, because he is copping the full brunt of my frustration.

In the lift queue, which is full of shiny, chatty, not-scared people, who I immediately hate, I realise I have to catch the triple chair as it comes around and we have to ride it as a threesome—Edwin, me and some cocky snowboarder who is totally absorbed by whatever noise is being pumped through his state-of-the-art headphones. And if I fuck it up the whole lift stops and everyone gets really pissed off. Edwin tells me to relax, but I am scared stiff, literally, my knees locked solid. We're next up and the first thing I do as the chair arrives is try to sit down, which I have been told expressly not to do. Edwin manages to catch me, wrangle me into position and then we are off, floating high above pristine slopes, skis dangling in thin air. It's beautiful, but all I can focus on is the impending dismount.

'Now,' Edwin says as my skis reconnect with snow, and

he expertly steers me by the elbow off to the left and out of harm's way. The fact that I don't bring anyone down feels like a major victory. Now that I'm up here I just have to learn to ski. Edwin leaves that monumental task to Eric from Austria, while he goes off in search of black runs and bumps.

By mid-afternoon I have mastered Wombat's Ramble, a gentle home trail that nevertheless feels like the Matterhorn to me. The first few times I tackle it with Eric skiing backwards in front of me and holding my hands while instructing me when to upweight, downweight, dig in my edges, face into the slope to turn and how to stop safely. And when my hour with Eric is up, I ski the trail three more exhilarating times on my own, riding the chair without incident, falling gracelessly many times over, but getting up as I've been taught and getting down safely to the basin, each time performing a small fist pump that I make sure no one else sees and channelling rivers of nervous sweat inside my super-heated Michelin-man ski suit. I decide it's time to stop when I register exhaustion that feels like the onset of anaesthesia. My head, my body, my brain—they all want out for a couple of hours before the others arrive. Somehow, I find my way to my bed and fall into deep, blissful sleep.

That night the chalet reverberates with English accents and laughter and reminiscences and overblown boasts and plans for tomorrow and boys eager to try black runs. Sandy and Conrad are the first of Edwin's friends I'm introduced to, even Edwin hasn't seen them since he visited them in England six years ago with his former partner, so this is a gamble for all of us. The boys, now gangly adolescents, Conrad hyper-energetic as Edwin promised he would be, Sandy serenely herding her cats, me a completely unknown quantity to them, and all of us crammed into a very small space. But my Syrian chicken is a hit, and the wine loosens any last vestiges of reserve and before bed we make a toilet rule that, if possible, shits will be taken offsite.

On our last day, Edwin wants to take me 'over the back'. We can get there on blue runs and he thinks I'm ready. He lures me with the mention of Maggie's Cafe which is right out in the middle of nowhere. I lose count of the number of times I fall on the way, and I curse my ageing knees for their lost ability to perform an effortless vertical lift, but when we eventually make it, the cafe is in chaos. The queues are long and the manager has apparently been gone for ages in search of fresh supplies, because they have run low on everything. No problem, we order a couple of toasties and coffees and sit out in the sun, happy to wait and recuperate.

Then I see the manger pull up on a snowmobile. It's Rudy! I almost dislocate my shoulder as I turn away, bury my face in my ski jacket and ask Edwin to go in when our order is called.

When he comes back, he says, 'Are you okay? What just happened?'

Then I tell him everything, because I can.

Sadly, I'm never going to make the Winter Olympics team, not even the veterans, but the ski trip is a huge success. I loved seeing Edwin so easy and relaxed around his friends, especially the boys, who he patiently taught to play five hundred, ensuring they wouldn't feel left out. I loved watching his effortlessly shooshy style on the slopes. I especially loved being taken right out of my comfort zone, and living to tell the tale.

On the way home we fizz with happy memories and I lament not taking up skiing when I was younger.

'How come you didn't?' Edwin asks.

'Because I was a reverse snob and I thought it was a sport for rich kids and wankers.'

'That's not completely untrue,' he says, 'but I learned to ski as a student at Huntingdale Tech and that was a long way from posh. The principal drove us up in his clapped-out old van, eight unruly year-nine boys, gave us a few basic tips and set us loose on the slopes. It was the first time I felt part of something, like I fitted in, and it was the first thing I was actually good at.'

Next morning, with recalcitrant muscles and moaning limbs, we head off to our respective jobs.

Me, to my new workplace, still alongside Eliza, but we're employees again, with male bosses again, and the adjustment is harder than I imagined. Since the merger I'm finding motivation increasingly hard to muster and my inspiration for finding new ways to flog stuff seriously on the wane. After thirty-five years I'm ready to try something new. The main reason I turn up every day is for Eliza, and the main reason I have hung in after being ready to retire at sixty is because, after the devastation of the split, the familiarity of our tight little team offered a safe and stable piece of ground in a landscape of shifting tectonic plates. But it's not fair to Eliza to just show up and go through the motions. She deserves better than that. I resolve to talk to her and put my exit plans back on the agenda.

Edwin, on the other hand, is committed to his business and his clients. He has a long-term lease on his city studio. He is doing the only work he knows, and he is quite a few years away from retirement.

Since he split with his former partner, Edwin has been renting a room from his friends in Brunswick, an arrangement which came with a predetermined end date of Christmas this year, so we nominate Christmas time, four months away, as our time to take stock and see where our relationship has landed. There will be the pros and cons of living together to be considered, whether we're ready for that and, if we are, where that might be. I've also earmarked December as my last month at work, which thrills me, but also terrifies me, especially when people ask, 'What are you going to do with all that free time?' and I have no ready answer. Finally, there's the fear, which still visits me regularly, of fucking up the rest of my life.

It's now over a year since Rex and I separated. I have filed for divorce, not because I have any intention of ever marrying again, but because it will signify the certainty of our severance and formally reinstate my independence. With much administrative effort, I have reverted to my maiden name, which I always liked much better than my married name anyway. I only took Rex's name in an obverse attempt to piss off my feminist friends, and because it was becoming increasingly popular at the time to take joint surnames, which I thought was even more unreasonable when you considered how that might extrapolate into future generations.

Today is the first day of spring, I'm sitting alone on my orange sofa and my thoughts have turned to love. It's a concept I'm finding more and more difficult to get my head around.

I think back to the instant when Rex told me he was seeing someone else, and the first question I asked, 'Do you love her?'

His answer was, 'Whatever that is—yes, I guess I do.' (I didn't realise until I watched *The Crown* that he'd stolen that line from Prince Charles.)

On hearing that, I'd thought, 'Perfect answer, because

clearly you have no idea what love is.' Nevertheless, in the moment, the admission murdered me.

Now twelve months later I'm more inclined to think that perhaps Rex's answer was not him being disingenuous. He knew he had feelings for Anna, but I don't think he'd worked out where that left me, us. He hadn't thought through the consequences of his actions or what would follow after the affair became known. He sent me an apologetic text acknowledging as much, saying how hurtful it must have been to receive news of the betrayal, then have to pack up and leave and face friends with the news.

There's no question that I loved Rex. I'd have done anything for him, tried always to please him, felt grateful that I had him in my life, felt proud of him, looked forward to seeing him, wanted him all to myself, at times even idolised him. But there's so much deference in that list and I wonder, is that what love is all about, and did that love simply become a habit I couldn't break? I compare that to how I feel about Edwin, which is probably unfair, because our love is still new, not properly set yet, and not tested by the wear of time, but the fundamentals on which it is based are very different. By his own admission Edwin is low maintenance, easy to please, cheap to keep. He is as uncomplicated as Rex was difficult, agreeable to the point of frustration, making me wish occasionally that he would put his foot down or express an emphatic preference. Still, the simplicity of our day-to-day existence and the clear air that it carries are a huge part of my attraction to Edwin.

On the back wall of the mezzanine space in the urban chalet that Edwin and I now share, there is a desk where I am writing this book, and, above it, a pinboard. The pinboard is crammed with the cuttings, snippets, thoughts, cards and photos I have collected since my world imploded. As I look at it now, I realise it represents a time capsule of an almost two-year journey. The highs and the lows.

First thing I ever pinned on that board was the receipt from Harvey Norman for my very own smart TV, a potent symbol of my independence—$1550 was never better spent.

Now they're all overlapping each other and curling at the corners. I look more closely.

There's a reproduction of the Paul Keating portrait at the National Parliament, given to me by Francie with the inscription: *We'll always have Paris, Jo, Love Paul xx*

An aphorism by Nayyirah Waheed called 'Circumstances' that I copied down on a scrap of paper: *'Where you are is not who you are.'* The 'Fuck Your Anxiety' card that came with Edwin's first bunch of lilies.

My work colleague Inga's pencil sketch of Rex with severed penis, bleeding scrotum and lifeless balls.

Albert Camus's quote about summer.

Leunig's 'Prayer to Self' clipped from a Saturday *Age*.

A desiccated dragonfly with gossamer wings intact that

I found in the Botanic Gardens on one of my many walks in the lost early days. It's a beautiful fragile thing, frozen in time.

A card from Genevieve and Sven showing a terrified Janet Leigh under the inscription: *Better to have loved and lost, than live with a psycho for the rest of your life!*

And one from Samantha the hairdresser:

> Dearest Jo,
> My newest but so special friend. We have been through shit. But look what grew from that. Happy Birthday. Love Samantha and Sashie [her dog, now my god-dog]

A gold-embossed Versace notecard, on which my GP (who practised until she was ninety-one and passed away during the writing of this book) had transcribed one of her original poems to present to me during a routine pap smear.

> Just
> Standing
> Enfolded in arms
> Is today, tomorrow or sometime
> Stillness, comfort and joy
> But
> Just
> Being
> Enfolded in mind
> Is timeless, boundless, universal
> Peace and sheer ecstasy.

The biggest surprise is that Edwin, the tailor-come-scientist-come-maker-and-fixer, is also an amateur artist and poet. On my pinboard, there are five poems penned 'when the muse was with him' during our early days. This is my favourite:

Algorithm of Animus
Take a sum over history
Of two perpendicular lives
And minds meeting equally,
Multiply by humour.
Subtract fear and entanglement
Divide its total by time.
Factor the attraction of two orbiting bodies
Justify with intimacy and touch.
Express the total as a pair,
Share the longing and trust.
Function with the harmonic
Revel in the symmetric
Calculate the remainder
Bracket it with care
Distribute the totalled bliss
By infinity
To share.
To Jo
Love Edwin

Eventually Edwin meets all my friends. They tell me they love him. They tell me he is good for me. I sense they mean it. We move in together. We meet each other's families. I retire and find purpose and pleasure in writing for myself rather than in response to client briefs. He keeps working at his studio in the city and riding his bike in all weather. It's a squeeze fitting all our stuff into one small apartment, and I've encouraged him to embrace the wisdom of Marie Kondo. Nevertheless, he continues to bring home orphans and outcasts found on the side of the road. It's not a straight line to relationship success; there are bumps and bends along the way, which we negotiate with an openness that I hope will remain a mainstay of our relationship for as long as we last.

Our best moments are always during our morning bubble, when we wake up, hold each other tummy to tummy and talk about anything and everything. It's the moment of suspension before the day takes hold.

Yesterday I said to him, 'I feel like we've gone next level.' And he said, 'Me too.'

ENDING #1

Full circle

28 February 2020. Today I met Rex at Guilfoyle's Volcano in the Botanic Gardens.

Earlier in the week, my friend Anthea, who works for a big real-estate agency, texted me to say, 'Guess whose house I wrote up this morning?'

I figured it must have been someone I knew, a local celebrity perhaps, so my guesses included George Colombaris (who was in the news at the time, for all the wrong reasons) and Ned who owned the heaving bakery on the corner of our street.

Then the penny dropped. Of course! It was my house, our house, now Rex's house. Anthea told me that when she arrived to do the walk-through and he opened the door, she nearly fell through the floor. Anthea was one of the friends I had lost regular contact with during the latter years with Rex, so she hadn't recognised the address. She quickly regained her composure and launched into professional mode, taking notes and highlighting selling points, putting the large landscaped rear garden at the top of her list. Then in the course of their conversation, Rex told her that he and his new partner were selling up to move north (another one of our retirement plans), knowing, surely, that this news would find its way back to me.

When Anthea and I spoke, after she'd told me how much she liked my old house, especially the garden, I asked her how Rex had seemed. 'Pretty good,' she said, 'his usual chatty self.' I asked how he looked. 'Also pretty good, unfortunately,' she said.

I was glad of Anthea's intelligence, but the news produced an unexpected jolt. Rex had been out of my life for three years, but subconsciously I knew he was still just down the road. Accessible. I don't know what comfort that gave me. Truth be told, I'd be better off with him and Anna interstate, because it would remove the possibility of accidentally running into them. But in some strange way I still felt proprietorial toward Rex, like he was mine but on some kind of extended loan to Anna. After all, there was so much of me in him now. I take credit for smoothing and shaping the boy from Frankston—expanding his appreciation of film (before he met me his favourite film was *Caddy Shack*), his interest in art and architecture with first-hand tutorials in Europe's finest galleries and cathedrals, his mode of dress, now verging on stylish—and that gave me some sense of ownership.

I sat on it for a while and then decided that if I was ever going to see Rex again, the time had come. I was in a good place. I felt strong and happy and keen to let go of the anger I'd been holding on to for the last three years. Of course, there were darker motivations too. I wanted to see how he was travelling, whether he was happy, if he felt like he'd made a huge mistake and, mostly, if he missed me.

I texted him:

> I've heard you are selling the house and heading north. I wonder if we should meet before you go and have a debrief of our life together and since. A kind of marriage post-mortem. I'm not sure it's a great idea. Sometimes I think so, sometimes not. Your thoughts??

His reply came back quick as a flash:

> Like you, I'm not sure, but agree it seems crazy to simply pretend thirty years together didn't happen. It would be good to catch up x

Just prior to that, I had been reading over some notes I took when I was in Bali at the yoga retreat not long after we split. We were all invited to attend a Buddhist temple ceremony. Apart from enjoying the beauty and serenity and other-worldliness of sitting in the light misting rain listening to the chanting and the service, I found the words nourishing. So much so, that when I returned to my room, I wrote down everything I could remember.

> Do not hold on to ill feeling; it will only create more damage.
> Be willing to forgive all mistakes, yours and others. This will free you.
> Do not waste time in bad situations. If they can't be fixed, move on.
> Only by accepting full responsibility for who we are, and whatever happens to us, can we hope to change our destiny.

Okay, they sound a bit clichéd now, but in the same way that every song feels like it was written for you when you're going through a breakup, I had felt, back then, that the great Buddha was talking directly to me and trying to tell me something.

When I first see Rex walking towards me, he looks older. Smaller. I recognise the singular gait conditioned by years of injuries and surgeries on his ankles, knees, shoulders and back. It speaks of time. Time we had spent together. Intimacies we had shared. He was always at his most loving post-anaesthesia. Happy to be alive. Happy to see me. A wave of panic swirls in my gut, brought on by nerves and the notion that this man, who I had been closer to than anyone for longer than anyone, was now a stranger to me.

I want to turn and run in the opposite direction, but it's too late, and when we greet each other the feeling subsides. It's as if I'm a performer consumed by dread just before walking on stage, but as soon as I deliver my opening lines, I'm okay.

We embrace stiffly, then as we walk along the meandering paths of the gardens we catch up on the recent developments in our lives and the world. Work, family, the mysterious virus surfacing in Wuhan. I'm comforted by the fact that I feel no sense of yearning towards him, that time has done its work. Yet I remain wildly curious to know how he really is, how his new life is panning out, who has fared better since the separation. I have questions that must be asked, so I suggest a coffee in the cafe by the lake.

Once we are settled at our outdoor table, shooing seagulls fighting over scraps, I dive into deeper water.

'What's it like sharing your life with someone so young?'

'Challenging. Awkward. People don't get it.'

He's aware that he is judged as a cliché. Older man, younger girl. Mid-life crisis on show for all to see.

He says their social life revolves around the bowling club. That those people are their community and to a large extent their friends. I guess this is no surprise—he was already well entrenched with them before we split. The bigger question is how Anna deals with it, how she fits in with this crowd. There is no one at the bowling club even close to her age, and surely there must be mutterings and insinuations about the 'appropriateness' of their relationship.

He tells me about her family and admits that when they go out with her mum, people assume that he and the mum are the couple and Anna is their daughter. He says this to me as a simple fact, but behind the telling I think I detect a ray of smug.

He admits he misses his old friends, but feels harshly judged by them. He takes refuge in the idea that if they can't get past what he had done, what he asserts millions of men before him had done, and the life that he has chosen, then they were never good friends anyway. I let that go, because I understand that this is the way he can rationalise his actions to himself and mitigate his distress at being abandoned by some of his oldest friends.

I ask about his depression. He says his medication is working and that mostly he feels good. I am pleased that he has been able to pull himself out of the hole he was in before we fell apart. He jokes about the fact that he has become a better and more fun person to live with. That he now drinks champagne and spirits (he would only drink beer and wine when he was with me). That he loves television series, has bought a new TV especially to watch them: *Better Call Saul, Mary Kills People*. That he's planning trips and life changes because, he acknowledges, I was right all along with my 'Last Viable Decade' theory; he feels it now that he's sixty-five—halfway through that decade we had earmarked as the one to get bucket-list things done, while the mind was still sharp and the body still willing.

There's a big floppy golden retriever eyeing us both as our coffees and scones arrive. 'I miss our dogs,' I say.

'One of the best things we did,' he replies.

A comfortable silence settles as we sip our lattes and look across at the lotus flowers on the lake. It feels like our initial reticence has thawed enough for me to risk the question I am most curious to ask—is he happy?

He dissembles, considers his answer carefully, because for him, too, this is a loaded question.

Finally, diplomatically, he says he cannot afford regret, that since the breakup with me he feels a deep and unshiftable sadness. I look at his face. This feels honest, like it has been offered at some considerable personal cost and even though I was secretly hoping for an answer like that, hearing it makes me a little sad too. The acknowledgment of our mutual loss.

I ask what he thinks went wrong with us. He says, 'Somewhere along the line, I just lost it. I could no longer grasp our dream. I let myself drift into a deep depression, and had no will to pull myself out.'

So, my theory was right: instead of recognising and treating the illness, which may have saved us, he'd opted to treat the symptoms. Medicating himself with the attentions of a girl who made him feel better. Special. Probably youthful again.

I exhale, realising that during that whole dialogue I had been holding my breath. Not fully aware of the weight those questions held for me today. How long they had rubbed away at my subconscious needing to be known? And I am satisfied, I have it now, not from a therapist or from my friends or from my own imagination, but from the horse's mouth. I can put that to rest.

Buoyed now by his honesty, I ask how come, for so long, I had to live with 'no fun' Rex. He's at a loss to explain this himself, but he at least acknowledges the truth of it. That he did cut himself off from me. That he made our life difficult and shut down the good times. He even admitted that his default position was 'No'.

This is a little victory for me, at least a vindication that I didn't imagine it. That the retreat was real. That, too, saddens me and I fleetingly wonder where we might be now if we'd managed the whole thing differently. Living out our retirement dreams in Europe? Perhaps, but then again, perhaps we'd both exhausted the possibilities for gratification from a life with each other.

The longer we talk, the more naturally the dialogue flows. We reminisce about our amazing adventures, getting stuck on a rock face in Italy while making a hair-raising chain-link traverse across the expanse with only dubious footholds, during which my phone fell from my pocket and plummeted hundreds of metres into the Mediterranean below. Terrifying at the time, but intrepid in the retelling and compensated for afterwards by the best spaghetti marinara of the trip. We relive our perilous ride along the narrow coast road in Corsica, having to negotiate oncoming tourist buses by pressing ourselves and our bikes hard against the cliff rather than risk the death drop on the other side. We talk about the joy of raising our beautiful puppies and the pain of letting them go. Rex informs me that Heather has been paired with an independently living blind woman and that they are flourishing together. I can't help but feel pride. Our girl. As the ease grows, and our memories glow, I can see he's getting a little teary, that maybe he's understanding what he sacrificed and feeling that what he gained is not equal to the loss. (Or is that just my take, what I wanted to see and hear? That's entirely possible.)

We finish our coffee and finger up the last crumbs of our scones, before making our way back to the Volcano gate. We stand together on the Tan track at the top of the Anderson Street hill, which we used to race up all those years ago, near where his car is parked.

'A new car,' I remark, but he doesn't bite.

When it's time to part, he is reluctant. He finds ways to stall, asks for book recommendations. Films. He asks if we can do it again, even asks if he can meet Edwin. When I tell him I don't think that's a good idea, he looks forlorn, his head hung low, his trademark smile absent, and I almost find myself feeling sorry for him. But then I remember Rex is the master manipulator. If he wants me to feel sorry for him, he knows how to do it.

Then out of the blue, as if to prove he still cares, and to hold me a bit longer, he says, 'You know you are still in my will. I haven't changed it.'

'What? Why?'

This is after he fought tooth and nail to extract as much from me as he possibly could.

'Well, to be fair, Jo, it's your money. You earned it.'

And that just floors me. Because there at last is the acknowledgment that never came when I needed it most, when we were negotiating our financial settlement, that I had been the major breadwinner most of our married life, and that towards the end I had stacked our retirement fund with my hard-earned bonuses for our joint benefit, to realise our lifelong dream, only to have it redirected at the cruellest of times to him and his new partner.

With this I am struck, not for the first time, by the notion that often Rex just doesn't see himself, or refuses to evaluate his actions, except through his own myopic lens. How does he think that admission makes me feel, coming three years too late and so casually offered. Is it supposed to be a consolation? And what am I supposed to do with that information now. I respond by saying, 'I'd prefer not to have to wait till you die to receive my fair share, Rex. Then again, I guess I could just kill you now and speed things up.'

And without trying to be glib he says, 'No need to be like that, Jo.'

As if I'm being unreasonable, or ungrateful.

I stand and watch as he drives off down the hill in his brand new Audi 4WD, white of course, then I walk up Domain Road back to my little urban chalet, reflecting on the revelations of this day. I think I've done Buddha proud. I know I've done myself proud. Even after the bizarre way our meeting concluded, I didn't let anger or accusation hijack the conversation. I even managed a little joke in the face of Rex's pitiful peace offering. I feel light on my feet, almost like I could break into a run, if only my knees would let me. The grand homes of South Yarra, the elite school, the manicured gardens don't rankle with their showy displays of privilege the way they sometimes do. Today they are incidental to the way I am feeling, a pretty backdrop to a satisfying sense of closure.

I have had my day of reckoning and it has delivered quite a few surprises. The good times, of which there were many, I'll now be able to bank and remember more fondly, knowing they were genuinely and mutually enjoyed. The bad times, of which there were also many and not of my imagination, are now consigned to history, acknowledged and endured by us both, a necessary part of what makes a partnership worth having. Yet as I float home through the sunlit streets, I know, beyond doubt, that my addiction is cured. That in the end, Rex has actually given me a gift. Admittedly, it was badly wrapped in lies, betrayal, anger and hurt, but once I peeled those layers away, there was something incredibly precious inside. My freedom and a second chance.

There's a certain symmetry to ending here. Closing the circle. You can imagine the film direction:

> *Cut to final scene:* Jo walks happily away from the man she so reluctantly left in the beginning. Camera follows her from behind as she gets smaller in frame and the world around her gets bigger. A godlike ray of sun bisects the image.
> *Screen title:* THE BEGINNING
> *Roll credits...*
> (Naturally, Guy Pearce will be appearing in the role of Edwin and maybe Claudia Karvan will play me, though she is a little young.)

But I don't want this story to end with Rex.

ENDING #2

Blackbird

Here's a sentence I never expected to write.

I am sixty-three years old and this morning I had the best sex of my life.

Edwin has a habit of waking early and an even better habit of using his beautiful Lamarckian hands to rouse me from sleep to semi-consciousness.

He does it slowly and unconditionally. It is not foreplay. It is not a signal that something is going to happen. But sometimes it just does.

And that's what happened today.

I was lying on my back, asleep, when I felt long slow circles of pressure on my stomach. They registered somewhere in my consciousness, and I lay there unmoving, letting it continue, willing it to continue. Later, how much later I couldn't tell you, I turned on my side so we were facing each other, our tummies touching. His hands moved to my back and kept circling.

I kept schtum. Feigning sleep, lapping it up, loving it. Then he produced the Octopus. The Octopus is our name for a signature technique of Edwin's where he softly clasps a handful of my skin, lifts it and lets it fall. Like a hungry octopus sucking food from a rock with its mouth. I love the Octopus, so in order not to disturb his feeding, I still didn't stir.

Let me tell you, that underwater garden is a blissful place to be.

After a long time, long enough for me to feel like I was taking advantage, I opened one eye, acknowledging my presence in this play.

He smiled, his crooked tailor smile that I first saw on Tinder and have loved ever since.

I lifted my arm and held it in the air. My skin was saggy and my hands were spotty and veined.

'I'm becoming an old lady,' I said.

'You're beautiful,' he said.

'Okay, a beautiful *old* lady,' I said.

'A sexy beautiful lady,' he replied looking me straight in the face and meaning it. He caressed my breasts and a surprise tear slid down my cheek.

Our hands kept touching, circling, providing pleasure and ease. I felt so relaxed I wanted to close my eyes and drift back into the ocean, to the depths of the Octopus's garden, to sleep. But I didn't, because I saw another smile cross Edwin's face and I registered the absolute privilege of having a man, one who might truly love you, lying beside you, expecting nothing, just giving. New territory for me.

I pressed close, trying to express my gratitude through touch, and felt his penis, patient, semi-erect, unexpectant. We'd reached a tipping point now—we both knew that, but still the pace didn't quicken. It remained languid, only the intention shifted.

We kissed. We pressed, we kissed some more. His penis was harder now and I massaged it with my thighs, but our eyes never unlocked. We kept looking at each other like we'd just found buried treasure.

As I lay on my back, Edwin rose above me in a perfect plank, obscuring the daylight from my view, filling it instead with his kind, craggy face. Rod Stewart's 'Maggie May' popped into my head and I was grateful for the human shield, blocking my lined face from the morning sun.

Our eventual lovemaking was organic, otherworldly, binding in a way that I'd never experienced before. The word 'sex' feels too base to describe it. Something hormone-fuelled teenagers might do, or married couples, on remote. But here we were, young lovers in old bodies, freed from our pasts. Sharing our bed with eros.

As we lay there afterwards lost in our private post-coital thoughts, we heard a blackbird singing. Edwin, my lover, lover also of nature and science, constant listener and keen observer, said, 'Our blackbird's back.' He'd been absent all the long winter months and we'd missed his morning wake-up calls. But here he was again, filling our morning with joy.

Acknowledgments

First, I want to acknowledge my friends. I can't thank you enough for being in my life. One reader said she saw my memoir as a beautiful tribute to female friendship. And I am so happy if that's the impression I leave, because friends are my lifeblood.

Thanks also to the people who became friends during the writing process. To my first critical reader Maha Sidaoui who did me the great favour of hooking me up with writer and editor Lyn Yeowart. I'm so grateful to you, Lyn, for picking me up and pushing me forward.

My first rejection was not all bad, but the suggestion that I fictionalise my story seemed to miss the whole point, so the manuscript languished in a bottom drawer, until I found mentor and memoir specialist Lee Kofman, who gave me just enough encouragement to keep going. She then set me a list of enormously daunting tasks, starting with a complete restructure. I am indebted to you, Lee, for seeing the writer in me and bringing my story to life.

I started writing this book when I was sixty. But it was not finished till I was sixty-six. My long-time friend Lisa

Chambers, who has a gift for making things happen, asked a friend who worked at Text if she would do a favour and read it. Now I have Lisa and Text to thank for making my dreams come true.

To publisher Michael Heyward, who confessed he dropped the book during the massage scene, thanks for reading and revelling in my antics. I wondered if a man would ever be a fan and you gave me a resounding yes. Thanks to Emily Booth, Lisa's friend, who did in fact read my manuscript and share it with her colleagues, and to Maddy Corbel, my publicist, who even as a young reader said she found so much to relate to in my story.

And to Jane Pearson, my editor at Text. Now that I actually know what an editor does, I understand why they are always the most effusively thanked people in these pages. Their job is to make writers sound so much better than they really are. And Jane you have done that for me. But more than that, you've been a pleasure to work with and made the polishing process a joyous education in grammar, punctuation, tense and tone.

In my first meeting at Text when I was rendered largely speechless by the occasion, I did manage to say, 'I think I've found my tribe.' And I had. Thanks to everyone at Text for making a newcomer feel so welcome and wanted.

Lastly to the man you know as Edwin. My wish would be that everyone could have an Edwin in their life. Thanks H, for finding me, encouraging me and truly loving me.